Christmas

Recipes & Crafts

Christmas
Recipes & Crafts

FOR THE PERFECT
HOME-MADE CHRISTMAS

This edition published by Parragon Books Ltd in 2015
LOVE FOOD is an imprint of Parragon Books Ltd

Parragon Books Ltd
Chartist House
15–17 Trim Street
Bath BA1 1HA, UK
www.parragon.com/lovefood

ISBN 978-1-4723-9253-4

Printed in China

Project managed by Annabel King
Introduction by Robin Donovan
New crafts by Clare Lloyd
New recipe photography by Mike Cooper
New craft and incidental photography by Henry Sparrow
Cover photography by Ian Garlick
Edited by Fiona Biggs

Title font: Saint Agnes © Great Lakes Lettering

Notes for the Reader

This book uses both metric and imperial measurements. Follow the same units of measurement throughout; do not mix metric and imperial. All spoon measurements are level: teaspoons are assumed to be 5 ml, and tablespoons are assumed to be 15 ml. Unless otherwise stated, milk is assumed to be full fat, eggs and individual vegetables are medium, pepper is freshly ground black pepper and salt is table salt. Unless otherwise stated, all root vegetables should be peeled prior to using.

The times given are an approximate guide only. Preparation times differ according to the techniques used by different people and the cooking times may also vary from those given.

For best results, use a food thermometer when cooking meat. Check the latest government guidelines for current advice.

Contents

Introduction

There's no denying it. Christmas is a truly magical time of year. There's the crisp, cool bite of winter air, the smell of pine needles, twinkling lights and, if you're lucky, even a few jingle bells jingling, too. And that's just outside. Inside cosy homes everywhere, the smells of freshly baked mince pies and biscuits mingle with the scent of the freshly cut Christmas tree adorned with twinkling lights, sparkling baubles and decorations. A gammon or a bird roasting in the oven raises everyone's appetite for the big sit-down meal that draws generations of family, loved ones and good friends to the table.

What better way to spend time with the family than cooking up delicious treats, making gifts for others and fashioning your own unique Christmas decorations? As the weather turns chilly and the days get shorter, the weeks leading up to Christmas are the perfect time to start your craft projects – whether you're making gifts or home decorations.

Decorations like the Christmas Wreath or Decorative Jar make lovely gifts for those hard-to-buy-for people on your list. Home-made Christmas cards, like the Christmas Snowflake Card come in handy when it's time to put Christmas and New Year greetings in the post. Gift Tags and Gift Decorations, too, are both useful and a fun way to add a personal touch to your gift presentations.

Set a festive scene in your home with Handmade Stockings, Christmas Card Tree Decorations, a Country-style Garland and a Decorative Centrepiece. And if you're feeling romantic, don't forget to hang a sprig or two of mistletoe!

The best cold-weather activity of all just might be staying indoors and cooking up delicious treats – either to give as gifts or serve to guests. From the Christmas Kitchen offers plenty of delectable gift ideas. From Indulgent Peppermint Hot Chocolate Mix and Pistachio & Apricot Nougat to Christmas Ginger Thins and Nutty Peppermint Bark, there's a sweet treat to appeal to everyone on your list. Savoury options like Corn Relish or Mixed Nuts in Herbed Salt are sure to delight those who don't go for sugary treats.

Once your gifts are all wrapped up, it's time to plan for the festive meals. No matter what type of affair you envision, our festive recipes will do the season justice. The Christmas Favourites chapter includes essential recipes

for the main event – Festive Prawn Cocktail, Traditional Roast Turkey, Roast Pheasant, Chestnut & Sausage Stuffing, Golden Christmas Cake and many other seasonal favourites.

Brunch favourites like Christmas Spiced Pancakes, Asparagus & Egg Pastries and the always-popular Pain au Chocolat Cinnamon Rolls are sure to delight on Christmas morning.

Kick off a celebratory dinner with Chestnut & Pancetta Soup or Baked Oregano Lobster. For the main dish, choose from a traditional Prime Rib of Beef au Jus or Roast Monkfish with Boulangère Potatoes. Pair these with superb sides like Mashed Sweet Potatoes. Desserts like Cheesecake with Caramel Pecan Nuts or a Dark Chocolate Yule Log provide an elegant ending.

We've even got you covered for drinks and canapés, with recipes for Holiday Eggnog, Kir Royale, Stuffed Olives, Blinis with Prawns & Wasabi Cream and more.

A chapter on leftovers offers deliciously creative ideas for giving them a second life. Turn leftover roast turkey into Turkey Club Sandwiches, leftover roast chicken into Chicken & Dumplings, leftover ham into Ham & Leek Risotto and leftover potatoes and Brussels sprouts into Salmon & Potato Casserole.

Enjoy the Season

Christmas is meant to be full of joy and good fun, but too often we get bogged down in the work of it all. So many parties to plan – and attend! – so many meals to cook, gifts to buy or make and other tasks to attend to. A good plan of action can ensure that you'll enjoy the season to the utmost.

Start your crafting and shopping early – as soon as the mood strikes. The minute the weather turns chilly is the perfect time to start thinking about Christmas crafts. For gifts, the advice to start early is always useful, but if you wait until the last couple of weeks before Christmas you can take advantage of the pre-Christmas sales. Better yet, if you're really organized, shop during the January sales for next year's gifts. Even if you simply take

advantage of reductions on gift wrap, greeting and gift cards, Christmas tree ornaments, lights and other decorations, you'll cut down on last-minute chores and save money.

As for the big day itself – or any parties you plan to throw for the season – the first order of business is to decide what type of affair you want to host. Will it be a fancy black-tie soirée with champagne and caviar and guests in their finery? Or do you prefer a cosier, family dinner with roast turkey, mince pies and Christmas pudding? Of course there are a million options in between, including a casual cocktail party, a buffet party, a themed brunch or a formal sit-down dinner.

Once you've settled on the event, start getting organized:

- **Create a guest list:** Decide how many people you'll invite. Will it be an intimate dinner for family and friends or would you prefer an open house with dozens of guests?

- **Send invitations:** Everyone is pulled in many different directions during this busy season, so send invitations well in advance – 4–6 weeks is ideal – and ask for RSVPs by a stated deadline.

- **Decide on a menu:** Once you know how many people are coming, put together a scrumptious menu that will suit your crowd.

- *Make ahead:* Casseroles, soups, cookies and cakes can often be made ahead of time and stashed in the refrigerator for a day or two, or in the freezer for much longer. Soups like our Spiced Pumpkin Soup freeze well. Mini quiches, tartlets, most biscuits and cakes and cranberry sauce can be made well in advance and frozen until they're needed.

- *Order special food items:* Butchers sell out of their regular supply at this time of year, so be sure to order the meat you need – whether it's a giant turkey or a prime rib, or sausage meat for stuffing. If you plan to serve cake from a local bakery, this, too, should be ordered well in advance.

- *Map out a timeline for the preceding week:* Build a plan of action that starts at least a week in advance of your event. List tasks that can be tackled well ahead of time, such as purchasing any decoration items (candles, place cards etc.) or polishing the silver, and then move on to those items that must be accomplished closer to the event, such as shopping for ingredients. Plan which items you'll accomplish each day of the week leading up to the event.

- *Map out a day-of-event timeline:* To make sure you're ready to go when that first guest rings the bell, map out a timeline for the day of your event. Plan when to take foods out of the freezer to thaw, when to begin preheating your oven and when to pop the roast in.

- *Enjoy!* Once your party begins, relax and remember to enjoy the moment. If you've done the work ahead of time, your guests are sure to enjoy themselves and you should, too.

The most important – and truly the most magnificent – thing about the Christmas season is having a chance to celebrate the joy of the season with those you love. Embrace the crisp weather, the aromas and flavours, the colours and twinkling lights, and the utter joy of Christmas through crafts and recipes.

Christmas Favourites

✻ ✻ ✻ ✻ ✻

Spiced Pumpkin Soup

A deliciously warming and luxuriously creamy soup that's perfect to start off your Christmas dinner.

SERVES 4   PREP 20 MINS. PLUS COOLING   COOK 35–40 MINS

2 tbsp olive oil

1 onion, chopped

1 garlic clove, chopped

1 tbsp chopped fresh ginger

1 small red chilli, deseeded and finely chopped

2 tbsp chopped fresh coriander

1 bay leaf

900 g/2 lb pumpkin, deseeded and diced

600 ml/1 pint vegetable stock

salt and pepper (optional)

single cream and chopped fresh coriander, to garnish

1. Heat the oil in a large saucepan over a medium heat. Add the onion and garlic and cook for about 4 minutes, until slightly soft. Add the ginger, chilli, coriander, bay leaf and pumpkin and cook for a further 3 minutes.

2. Pour in the stock and bring to the boil. Skim any foam from the surface, if necessary. Reduce the heat and simmer, stirring occasionally, for about 25 minutes, or until the pumpkin is tender. Remove from the heat, remove and discard the bay leaf and leave the soup to cool.

3. Transfer to a food processor or blender, in batches if necessary, and process until smooth. Return the mixture to the rinsed-out pan and season to taste with salt and pepper, if using.

4. Reheat gently, then remove from the heat and pour into warmed soup bowls. Garnish each bowl with a swirl of cream and some chopped coriander and serve immediately.

Tip DON'T DISCARD THE PUMPKIN SEEDS, SIMPLY RINSE AND DRY THEM, THEN TIP ONTO A LINED BAKING TRAY AND TOSS WITH OIL AND SALT. COOK FOR 15 MINUTES IN AN OVEN PREHEATED TO 140°C/275°F/GAS MARK 1, UNTIL GOLDEN BROWN. THEY WILL MAKE A DELICIOUS AND HEALTHY SNACK.

1

2

3

Festive Prawn Cocktail

This classic starter has never lost its appeal. Creamy avocado and full-flavoured prawns are complemented by a hearty mayonnaise.

SERVES 8   PREP 25 MINS   COOK NONE

125 ml/4 fl oz tomato ketchup

1 tsp chilli sauce

1 tsp Worcestershire sauce

2 ruby grapefruits

8 lettuce leaves, shredded

1 kg/2 lb 4 oz cooked tiger prawns, peeled and deveined

2 avocados, peeled, stoned and diced

lime slices and fresh dill sprigs, to garnish

MAYONNAISE

2 large egg yolks

1 tsp English mustard powder

1 tsp salt

pinch of pepper

300 ml/10 fl oz groundnut oil

1 tsp white wine vinegar

1. To make the mayonnaise, put the egg yolks in a bowl, add the mustard powder, salt and pepper and beat together well. Begin whisking the egg yolks, adding the oil just one drop at a time, making sure that this has been thoroughly absorbed before adding another drop and whisking well.

2. Continue adding the oil one drop at a time until the mixture thickens and stiffens – at this point, whisk in the vinegar, then continue to dribble in the remaining oil very slowly in a thin stream, whisking constantly, until you have used up all the oil and you have a thick mayonnaise.

3. Mix the mayonnaise, tomato ketchup, chilli sauce and Worcestershire sauce together in a small bowl. Cover with clingfilm and refrigerate until required.

4. Cut off a slice from the top and bottom of each grapefruit, then peel off the skin and all the white pith. Cut between the membranes to separate the segments.

5. When ready to serve, make a bed of shredded lettuce in the bases of eight glass dishes. Divide the prawns, grapefruit segments and avocados between them and spoon over the mayonnaise dressing. Serve the cocktails garnished with lime slices and dill sprigs.

Traditional Roast Turkey

For many families, this magnificent bird is the centrepiece of the festive meal, usually served with roast potatoes, rich gravy and Brussels sprouts.

SERVES 4   PREP 25 MINS   COOK 3 HRS 15 MINS, PLUS STANDING

1 oven-ready turkey, weighing
5 kg/11 lb

1 garlic clove, finely chopped

100 ml/3½ fl oz red wine

75 g/2¾ oz butter

seasonal vegetables, to serve

STUFFING

100 g/3½ oz button
mushrooms, chopped

1 onion, chopped

1 garlic clove, chopped

85 g/3 oz butter

100 g/3½ oz fresh
breadcrumbs

2 tbsp finely chopped fresh
sage

1 tbsp lemon juice

salt and pepper (optional)

PORT & CRANBERRY
SAUCE

100 g/3½ oz sugar

275 ml/9 fl oz port

175 g/6 oz fresh cranberries

1. Preheat the oven to 200°C/400°F/Gas Mark 6.

2. To make the stuffing, put the mushrooms in a saucepan with the onion, garlic and butter and cook for 3 minutes. Remove from the heat and stir in the remaining stuffing ingredients. Fill the neck end of the turkey with the stuffing and truss with string.

3. Put the turkey in a roasting tin. Rub the garlic over the bird and pour the wine over. Add the butter and roast in the preheated oven for 30 minutes. Baste, then reduce the temperature to 180°C/350°F/Gas Mark 4 and roast for a further 40 minutes. Baste again and cover with foil. Roast for a further 2 hours, basting regularly. Check that the bird is cooked by inserting a knife between the legs and body. If the juices run clear, it is cooked. Remove from the oven, loosely cover with foil and leave to stand for 25 minutes.

4. Meanwhile, to make the sauce, put the sugar, port and cranberries in a saucepan. Heat over a medium heat until almost boiling. Serve the turkey with seasonal vegetables, if using, and the port and cranberry sauce.

Roast Pheasant

Pheasant can be a little dry but the herb butter that is pushed under the skin before cooking ensures a delicious, moist result.

100 g/3½ oz butter, slightly softened

1 tbsp chopped fresh thyme

1 tbsp chopped fresh parsley

2 oven-ready young pheasants

4 tbsp vegetable oil

125 ml/4 fl oz red wine

salt and pepper (optional)

GAME CHIPS

650 g/1 lb 7oz potatoes

sunflower oil, for deep-frying

1. Preheat the oven to 190°C/375°F/Gas Mark 5. Put the butter in a small bowl and mix in the thyme and parsley. Lift the skins off the pheasants, taking care not to tear them, and push the herb butter under the skins. Season to taste.

2. Pour the oil into a roasting tin, add the pheasants and roast in the preheated oven for 45 minutes, basting occasionally. Remove from the oven, pour over the wine, then return to the oven and cook for a further 15 minutes, or until cooked through. Check that each bird is cooked by inserting a knife between the legs and body. If the juices run clear, they are cooked.

3. To make the game chips, peel the potatoes and cut into wafer-thin slices. Immediately place in a bowl of cold water. Heat enough oil for deep-frying in a large saucepan or a deep fryer to 180–190°C/350–375°F, or until a cube of bread browns in 30 seconds. Drain the potato slices and pat dry with kitchen paper. Deep-fry, in batches, for 2–3 minutes, stirring to prevent them sticking, then remove with a slotted spoon. Drain on kitchen paper.

4. Remove the pheasants from the oven, loosely cover with foil and leave to rest for 15 minutes. Serve on a warmed serving platter surrounded by the game chips.

Yuletide Goose

The uncooked goose may seem very large, but it will lose a lot of fat during cooking, making it ideal to serve to a smaller number of guests.

SERVES 4–6   PREP 15 MINS   COOK 2 HRS 45 MINS–3 HRS 15 MINS

a 3.5–4.5-kg/7¾–10-lb
oven-ready goose
1 tsp salt
4 pears
1 tbsp lemon juice
4 tbsp butter
2 tbsp honey

1. Preheat the oven to 220°C/425°F/Gas Mark 7. Use a fork to prick the skin all over, then rub with the salt. Place the bird upside down on a rack in a roasting tin. Roast in the preheated oven for 30 minutes. Drain off the fat. Turn the bird over and roast for 15 minutes, then drain off the fat.

2. Reduce the oven temperature to 180°C/350°F/Gas Mark 4 and roast for 15 minutes per 450 g/1 lb. Cover with foil 15 minutes before the end of the cooking time. Check that the bird is cooked by inserting a knife between the legs and body. If the juices run clear, it is ready. Remove from the oven. Transfer the goose to a warmed serving platter, loosely cover with foil and leave to rest.

3. Meanwhile, peel and halve the pears, then brush with the lemon juice. Melt the butter and honey in a saucepan over a low heat, then add the pears. Cook, stirring, for 5–10 minutes until tender. Remove from the heat, arrange the pears around the goose and pour the sweet juices over the bird, then serve.

Seafood Pie with Stilton

For an alternative to meat on Christmas Day, a creamy seafood pie rings the changes. Stilton cheese adds a distinctly Christmassy flavour.

SERVES 6   PREP 30 MINS   COOK 1 HR

300 ml/10 fl oz vegetable stock

100 ml/3½ fl oz dry vermouth

3 tbsp cornflour, blended with 3 tbsp cold water

30 g/1 oz butter, cut into small pieces

6 tbsp crème fraîche

375 g/13 oz skinless cod fillet, cut into chunks

375 g/13 oz skinless salmon fillet, cut into chunks

225 g/8 oz raw king prawns, peeled and deveined

175 g/6 oz fine asparagus spears, tough ends snapped off, cut into 2.5-cm/1-inch pieces

115 g/4 oz Stilton cheese, crumbled

4 tbsp snipped fresh chives

500 g/1 lb 2 oz ready-made puff pastry

10 g/¼ oz plain flour, for dusting

pepper (optional)

1. Pour the stock and vermouth into a saucepan and bring to the boil. Whisk in the cornflour paste and simmer for 1 minute to make a thick sauce. Remove from heat and stir in the butter and crème fraîche, then cover the surface with baking paper. Leave to cool.

2. Preheat the oven to 220°C/425°F/Gas Mark 7. Stir the fish, prawns, asparagus, cheese and chives into the sauce. Season to taste with pepper, if using, then spoon into a 1.5-litre/2½-pint pie dish.

3. Roll out the pastry on a lightly floured surface to a thickness of 3 mm/⅛ inch. Cut a long 2-cm/¾-inch strip and press it around the rim of the pie dish, fixing it in place with a little water. Use the remaining pastry to cover the pie, cutting the trimmings into shapes to decorate and fixing into place with a little water. Make a small hole in the centre to allow steam to escape.

4. Bake in the preheated oven for 20 minutes, until the pastry is well risen and golden brown, then reduce the oven temperature to 180°C/350°F/Gas Mark 4 and bake for a further 35 minutes. Serve immediately.

Bacon-wrapped Sausages

These are traditionally served with the big Christmas meal – they certainly add something extra to the table when served around the Christmas turkey.

MAKES 8   PREP 15 MINS   COOK 15–20 MINS

8 pork sausages
2 tbsp mild mustard
24 ready-to-eat prunes
8 smoked bacon rashers

1. Preheat the grill. Using a sharp knife, cut a slit along the length of each sausage about three quarters of the way through. Spread the mustard inside the slits and press 3 prunes into each sausage.

2. Stretch the bacon with the back of a knife until each rasher is quite thin. Wrap a rasher of bacon around each sausage.

3. Place the sausages on a grill rack and cook under the grill, turning occasionally, for 15–20 minutes until cooked through and browned all over.

1

2

2

Chestnut & Sausage Stuffing

A substantial stuffing that is almost a meal in itself! It can be used to stuff the turkey or cooked separately and served alongside.

SERVES 6–8   PREP 10 MINS   COOK 30–40 MINS

225 g/8 oz pork sausage meat

225 g/8 oz unsweetened chestnut purée

85 g/3 oz walnuts, chopped

115 g/4 oz ready-to-eat dried apricots, chopped

2 tbsp chopped fresh parsley

2 tbsp snipped fresh chives

2 tsp chopped fresh sage

4–5 tbsp double cream

salt and pepper (optional)

1. Preheat the oven to 190°C/375°F/Gas Mark 5. Combine the sausage meat and chestnut purée in a bowl, then stir in the walnuts, apricots, parsley, chives and sage. Stir in enough cream to make a firm, but not dry, mixture. Season to taste with salt and pepper, if using.

2. If you are planning to stuff a turkey or goose, fill the neck cavity only to ensure the bird cooks all the way through. It is safer and more reliable to cook the stuffing separately, either rolled into small balls and placed on a baking sheet or spooned into an ovenproof dish.

3. Cook the separate stuffing in a preheated oven for 30–40 minutes at 190°C/375°F/Gas Mark 5. It should be allowed a longer time to cook if you are roasting a bird at a lower temperature in the same oven.

Rich Bread Sauce

This simple but deliciously rich sauce is a classic accompaniment to roast turkey, but is also good with other roast meats and game.

SERVES 12 | *PREP 15 MINS, PLUS INFUSING* | *COOK 20–25 MINS*

1 onion, peeled but left whole
12 cloves
1 bay leaf
6 peppercorns
600 ml/1 pint milk
115 g/4 oz fresh white breadcrumbs
25 g/1 oz butter
½ tsp grated nutmeg
2 tbsp double cream (optional)
salt and pepper (optional)
¼ tsp grated nutmeg and 1 bay leaf, to garnish

1. Make 12 small holes in the onion using a skewer or sharp knife and stick a clove in each hole.

2. Place the onion, bay leaf and peppercorns in a small saucepan and pour in the milk. Place over a medium heat, bring to the boil, remove from the heat, then cover and leave to infuse for 1 hour.

3. Strain the milk and discard the onion, bay leaf and peppercorns.

4. Return the milk to the rinsed-out pan and add the breadcrumbs. Cook the sauce over a very gentle heat until the breadcrumbs have swollen and the sauce is thick. Stir in the butter and season with salt and pepper, if using.

5. When ready to serve, reheat the sauce briefly, if necessary. Add the nutmeg and stir in the double cream, if using. Pour into a warmed serving bowl and serve immediately, garnished with a bay leaf and grated nutmeg.

Cauliflower Cheese

Delicious cauliflower cheese makes a welcome addition to the Christmas dinner table. Try adding broccoli as well for a tasty variation.

SERVES 4   PREP 10 MINS   COOK 20 MINS

1 cauliflower, cut into florets
(675 g/1 lb 8 oz prepared
weight)

40 g/1½ oz butter

40 g/1½ oz plain flour

450 ml/15 fl oz milk

115 g/4 oz Cheddar cheese,
finely grated

pinch of freshly grated nutmeg

1 tbsp freshly grated
Parmesan cheese

salt and pepper (optional)

1. Bring a saucepan of water to the boil, add the cauliflower, bring back to the boil and cook for 4–5 minutes. It should still be firm. Drain, place in a preheated 1.5-litre/2½-pint gratin dish and keep warm.

2. Melt the butter in the rinsed-out pan over a medium heat and stir in the flour. Cook, stirring constantly, for 1 minute. Remove from the heat and gradually stir in the milk until smooth.

3. Return to a medium heat and continue to stir while the sauce comes to the boil and thickens. Reduce the heat and simmer gently, stirring constantly, for about 3 minutes until creamy and smooth.

4. Remove from the heat and stir in the Cheddar cheese and nutmeg. Season to taste with salt and pepper, if using.

5. Preheat the grill to high. Pour the sauce over the cauliflower, top with the Parmesan cheese and place under a hot grill to brown. Serve immediately.

Rich Christmas Pudding

This pudding is one of the traditional stars of Christmas. Made in advance, it's like another present to unwrap on Christmas day!

SERVES 10–12   PREP 30 MINS. PLUS SOAKING   COOK 6 HRS. PLUS REHEATING

200 g/7 oz currants

200 g/7 oz raisins

200 g/7 oz sultanas

150 ml/5 fl oz sweet sherry

175 g/6 oz butter

175 g/6 oz brown sugar

4 eggs, beaten

150 g/5½ oz self-raising flour

100 g/3½ oz fresh breadcrumbs

50 g/1¾ oz blanched almonds, chopped

juice of 1 orange

grated rind of ½ orange

grated rind of ½ lemon

½ tsp mixed spice

10 g/¼ oz butter, for greasing

10 g/¼ oz icing sugar, for dusting

1. Put the currants, raisins and sultanas in a glass bowl and pour the sherry over. Cover and leave to soak for at least 2 hours.

2. Beat together the butter and brown sugar in a bowl. Beat in the eggs, then fold in the flour. Stir in the soaked fruit and the sherry with the breadcrumbs, almonds, orange juice, orange rind, lemon rind and mixed spice. Grease a 1.2-litre/2-pint pudding basin and spoon the mixture into it, packing it down well and leaving a gap of 2.5 cm/1 inch at the top. Cut a round of greaseproof paper 3 cm/1½ inches larger than the top of the basin, grease with butter and place over the pudding. Secure with string, then top with two layers of foil.

3. Place the pudding in a saucepan two-thirds filled with boiling water. Reduce the heat and simmer for 6 hours, topping up the water in the saucepan when necessary.

4. Remove from the heat and leave to cool. Replace the greaseproof paper and foil and store the pudding in a cool place for 2–8 weeks. To reheat, steam as before for 2 hours. Decorate with a dusting of icing sugar and serve.

Festive Mince Pies

Nothing says 'Christmas' more clearly than the traditional mince pie. Be generous with the mincemeat – these pies should be luscious!

SERVES 16   PREP 30 MINS   COOK 15 MINS, PLUS COOLING

10 g/¼ oz butter, for greasing

200 g/7 oz plain flour

100 g/3½ oz butter

25 g/1 oz icing sugar

1 egg yolk

2–3 tbsp milk

10 g/¼ oz flour, for dusting

300 g/10½ oz ready-made mincemeat

1 tbsp milk, for glazing

10 g/¼ oz icing sugar, for dusting

1. Preheat the oven to 180°C/350°F/Gas Mark 4. Grease a 16-hole tartlet tin with butter. Sift the flour into a bowl. Using your fingertips, rub in the butter until the mixture resembles breadcrumbs. Stir in the sugar and egg yolk. Stir in enough milk to make a soft dough, turn out onto a lightly floured work surface and lightly knead until smooth.

2. Shape the dough into a ball and roll out to a thickness of 1 cm/½ inch. Use fluted cutters to cut out 16 x 7-cm/2¾-inch rounds and use to line the holes in the prepared tin. Half-fill each pie with mincemeat. Cut out 16 star shapes from the leftover dough, brush with milk and place one on top of each pie.

3. Glaze the surface of the pies with milk and bake in the preheated oven for 15 minutes until the pastry is a pale golden colour. Remove from the oven and leave to cool on a wire rack. Dust with the icing sugar just before serving.

Golden Christmas Cake

This delicious fruit cake is a Christmas favourite. The secret of its success is the long storage before serving, so make ahead for the best results!

❧

SERVES 16–18   PREP 45 MINS, PLUS SOAKING   COOK 1½–2 HRS

175 g/6 oz dried apricots, chopped

85 g/3 oz dried mango, chopped

85 g/3 oz dried pineapple, chopped

175 g/6 oz sultanas

55 g/2 oz chopped stem ginger

55 g/2 oz chopped mixed peel

finely grated rind and juice of 1 orange

4 tbsp brandy

10 g/¼ oz butter, for greasing

175 g/6 oz butter

100 g/3½ oz light muscovado sugar

4 eggs, beaten

2 tbsp clear honey

175 g/6 oz self-raising flour

2 tsp ground allspice

85 g/3 oz pecan nuts, chopped

800 g/1 lb 12 oz marzipan

900 g/2 lb white ready-to-roll fondant icing

silver dragées, to decorate

1. Place the apricots, mango and pineapple in a bowl with the sultanas, ginger and mixed peel. Stir in the orange rind and juice and brandy. Cover and leave to soak overnight.

2. Preheat the oven to 160°C/325°F/Gas Mark 3. Grease a 23-cm/9-inch round springform cake tin and line with baking paper.

3. Cream together the butter and sugar until the mixture is pale and fluffy. Add the eggs to the mixture, beating well between each addition. Stir in the honey. Sift the flour with the allspice and fold into the mixture using a metal spoon. Add the soaked fruit and the nuts, mixing thoroughly. Spoon the mixture into the prepared tin, spreading evenly, then make a slight dip in the centre.

4. Bake in the centre of the preheated oven for 1½–2 hours, or until golden brown and firm to the touch and a skewer inserted into the centre of the cake comes out clean. Leave to cool in the tin.

5. Turn out the cake, remove the paper and wrap in clean baking paper and foil. Store in a cool place for at least 1 month before use. Cover the cake with marzipan and white ready-to-roll icing, following the packet instructions, then decorate with icing stars and silver dragées.

Crème Brûlée

This is crème brûlée with a twist – delicious soft fruit lies waiting to be discovered under the crisp caramelized topping and creamy layer beneath.

SERVES 6 — PREP 15 MINS — COOK 5 MINS, PLUS CHILLING

225–300 g/8–10½ oz mixed soft fruits, such as blueberries and stoned fresh cherries

1½–2 tbsp orange liqueur

250 g/9 oz mascarpone cheese

200 ml/7 fl oz crème fraîche

2–3 tbsp dark muscovado sugar

1. Place the fruit in the bases of six 150-ml/5-fl oz ramekin dishes. Sprinkle the fruit with the liqueur.

2. Cream the mascarpone cheese in a bowl until soft, then gradually beat in the crème fraîche.

3. Spoon the cheese mixture over the fruit, smoothing the surface and ensuring that the tops are level. Chill in the refrigerator for at least 2 hours.

4. Sprinkle the tops with the sugar. Using a chef's blow torch, grill the tops until caramelized (about 2–3 minutes). Alternatively, cook under a preheated grill, turning the dishes, for 3–4 minutes, or until the tops are lightly caramelized all over.

5. Serve warm or chill in the refrigerator for 15–20 minutes before serving.

Tip YOU COULD VARY THE FRUIT ACCORDING TO TASTE. SOFT FRUIT IS BEST, SO USE CHOPPED STONED FRESH APRICOTS, PEACHES OR PLUMS, OR A COMBINATION OF ANY OF THESE. FRUITS OF THE FOREST ARE ALSO A PERFECT COMPLEMENT TO THIS LUSCIOUS AND CREAMY DESSERT.

Christmas Morning

❋ ❋ ❋ ❋ ❋ ❋

Rich Orange Crêpes

If you like pancakes for breakfast, you'll love these light and luscious buttery crêpes, richly flavoured with juicy oranges on Christmas Day.

SERVES 4   PREP 15 MINS   COOK 10 MINS

150 g/5½ oz plain flour
200 ml/7 fl oz milk
1 large egg
3 tbsp fresh orange juice
2 tbsp melted butter
10 g/¼ oz melted butter, for frying
2 oranges, segmented, to serve

ORANGE BUTTER

55 g/2 oz unsalted butter
finely grated rind and juice of 1 orange
1 tbsp caster sugar

1. To make the crêpes, put the flour, milk, egg, orange juice and butter into a mixing bowl and whisk until smooth. Alternatively, whizz in a food processor until smooth.

2. Heat a crêpe pan until hot, lightly brush with melted butter and pour in a small ladleful of batter, swirling to thinly coat the surface of the pan.

3. Cook the crêpe until golden underneath, then turn and cook the other side. Repeat this process using the remaining batter, brushing the pan with butter as needed and keeping the cooked crêpes warm.

4. To make the orange butter, melt the butter in a small saucepan, add the orange rind and juice and the sugar and stir until the sugar has dissolved. Simmer, stirring, for 30 seconds, then remove from the heat.

5. Serve the crêpes folded over, with the orange segments and the orange butter poured over.

Apple & Spice Porridge

What better way to set yourself up for Christmas Day than with this delicious and wholesome porridge, full of warm, spicy goodness.

SERVES 4   PREP 5 MINS   COOK 15 MINS

600 ml/1 pint milk
1 tsp salt
115 g/4 oz medium rolled porridge oats
2 large apples
½ tsp ground mixed spice
clear honey, to serve

1. Put the milk in a saucepan and bring to the boil. Add the salt and sprinkle in the oats, stirring constantly.

2. Place over a low heat and leave the oats to simmer for 10 minutes, stirring occasionally.

3. Meanwhile, peel, halve, core and grate the apples. When the porridge is creamy and most of the liquid has evaporated, stir in the grated apple and mixed spice. Spoon into serving bowls and drizzle with honey.

Tip IF YOU DON'T LIKE THE RICH CREAMINESS OF PORRIDGE MADE WITH MILK, YOU CAN ALWAYS SUBSTITUTE IT WITH AN EQUAL QUANTITY OF WATER, AND JUST SERVE THE PORRIDGE WITH MILK OR CREAM FOR POURING. YOU COULD ALSO TRY SERVING IT WITH MAPLE SYRUP FOR A REALLY SWEET HIT.

1

2

3

Christmas
Spiced Pancakes

With Christmas flavours of cranberries and nuts and the indulgence of a rum-infused syrup, these pancakes are well worth making.

SERVES 4   PREP 10 MINS, PLUS STANDING   COOK 20 MINS

150 g/5½ oz plain flour

1½ tsp baking powder

pinch of salt

1 tsp mixed spice

275 ml/9 fl oz milk

1 large egg

2 tbsp melted butter

100 g/3½ oz cranberries, chopped

40 g/1½ oz chopped mixed peel

25 g/1 oz hazelnuts, chopped

1 tbsp sunflower oil, for oiling

2 tbsp soft dark brown sugar

60 ml/2 fl oz water

3 tbsp dark rum

1 tsp vanilla extract

1. Sift the flour, baking powder, salt and mixed spice into a bowl. Add the milk, egg and butter and whisk until smooth. Stir in the cranberries, mixed peel and hazelnuts and leave to stand for 5 minutes.

2. Lightly oil a griddle pan or frying pan and heat over a medium heat. Spoon tablespoons of the batter onto the pan to make oval shapes, and cook until bubbles appear on the surface.

3. Turn over with a palette knife and cook the other side until golden brown. Repeat this process using the remaining batter, while keeping the cooked pancakes warm.

4. Place the sugar and water in a small saucepan and heat over a low heat, stirring, until the sugar has dissolved. Bring to the boil and boil for 1 minute, then add the rum and vanilla extract and bring back to the boil. Remove from the heat.

5. Spoon the syrup over the pancakes and serve immediately.

Mushrooms & Sage on Sourdough Toast

Sourdough bread is very substantial, making this a really hearty breakfast if you have a long day of festivities ahead!

SERVES 4   PREP 10 MINS   COOK 10 MINS

5 tbsp olive oil

2 tbsp roughly chopped fresh sage, plus 16–20 whole small leaves

400 g/14 oz even-sized chestnut mushrooms, halved

squeeze of lemon juice

1 large garlic clove, thinly sliced

2 tbsp chopped fresh flat-leaf parsley

¼ tsp pepper

pinch of sea salt flakes

4 slices sourdough bread

Parmesan cheese shavings, to garnish

1. Heat the oil in a large frying pan over a medium–high heat. Add the chopped sage and sizzle for a few seconds. Add the mushrooms and fry for 3–4 minutes, or until they are beginning to release their juices.

2. Add the lemon juice, then add the garlic, parsley, pepper and salt. Cook for a further 5 minutes.

3. Meanwhile, toast the bread on both sides. Place on warmed plates and pile the mushrooms on top.

4. Sizzle the whole sage leaves in the oil remaining in the pan over a high heat for a few seconds, until crisp. Scatter over the mushrooms and garnish with cheese shavings.

Poached Eggs with Spinach & Cheddar

Guests coming for Christmas Day brunch? Serve this easy spin on eggs Florentine as a delicious yet simple festive treat.

SERVES 4   *PREP 10 MINS*   *COOK 15 MINS*

1 tbsp olive oil

200 g/7 oz young spinach leaves

4 thick slices ciabatta bread

25 g/1 oz butter

4 large eggs

100 g/3½ oz Cheddar cheese, grated

salt and pepper (optional)

freshly grated nutmeg, to serve

1. Preheat the grill to high. Heat the oil in a wok or large saucepan, add the spinach and stir-fry for 2–3 minutes until the leaves are wilted. Drain in a colander, season to taste with salt and pepper, if using, and keep warm.

2. Toast the bread on both sides until golden. Spread one side of each slice with butter and place buttered side up in a baking dish.

3. Meanwhile, fill a deep frying pan with boiling water and bring back to the boil. Reduce the heat to a gentle simmer. Break the eggs into the water and poach for 2–3 minutes until the whites are set. Remove from the pan with a draining spoon.

4. Arrange the spinach on the toast and top each slice with a poached egg. Sprinkle with the grated cheese. Cook under the preheated grill for 1–2 minutes until the cheese has melted. Sprinkle with nutmeg and serve immediately.

1

2

4

Smoked Salmon & Egg on Toasted Muffin

Topped with an easy no-fail hollandaise sauce, this is the ultimate festive brunch dish for two.

SERVES 2　　*PREP 20 MINS*　　*COOK 7–8 MINS*

4 eggs

2 English muffins

10 g/¼ oz butter, for spreading

15 g/½ oz rocket leaves

115 g/4 oz smoked salmon slices

HOLLANDAISE SAUCE

2 large egg yolks

2 tsp lemon juice

1 tbsp white wine vinegar

100 g/3½ oz unsalted butter

salt and pepper (optional)

1. To make the hollandaise sauce, place the egg yolks in a blender. Season with salt and pepper, if using, then process for a few seconds until thoroughly blended.

2. Place the lemon juice and vinegar in a small saucepan and heat until simmering. With the blender running, add the hot liquid in a slow, steady stream. Turn off the blender.

3. Place the butter in the pan and heat until melted and foaming. With the blender running, add the butter, a few drops at a time, until you have a smooth, thick sauce. Use a spatula to scrape down any sauce from the side of the blender, then whizz for a further few seconds.

4. Fill a deep frying pan with boiling water and bring back to the boil. Reduce the heat to a gentle simmer. Break the eggs into the water and poach for 2–3 minutes until the whites are set. Remove from the pan with a draining spoon. Split and lightly toast the muffins under a hot grill.

5. Spread the toasted muffins with the butter and place on two serving plates. Top with nearly all the rocket leaves and the slices of smoked salmon. Remove the eggs from the water with a slotted spoon, drain on kitchen paper and place on top of the salmon. Spoon the warm sauce over the poached eggs. Garnish with pepper, if using, and the remaining rocket leaves. Serve immediately.

Asparagus & Egg Pastries

Asparagus and eggs make a great pairing in any recipe. These quick and easy pastries would be great for a Christmas brunch buffet.

SERVES 4 · PREP 30 MINS, PLUS CHILLING · COOK 20 MINS

500 g/1 lb 2 oz ready-made puff pastry

10 g/¼ oz flour, for dusting

1 tbsp milk, for brushing

300 g/10½ oz slim asparagus spears

200 g/7 oz ready-made tomato pasta sauce

1 tsp hot smoked paprika

4 eggs

1. Roll out the pastry on a lightly floured surface to a 35 x 20-cm/14 x 8-inch rectangle, then cut into four 20 x 9-cm/8 x 3½-inch rectangles.

2. Line a baking sheet with non-stick baking paper and place the pastry rectangles on the sheet. Prick all over with a fork and brush lightly with milk. Chill in the refrigerator for 20 minutes.

3. Snap the woody ends off the asparagus and discard. Bring a saucepan of water to the boil. Add the asparagus, bring back to the boil and cook for 2–3 minutes, until almost tender. Drain and refresh in cold water, then drain again and set aside.

4. Meanwhile, preheat the oven to 200°C/400°F/Gas Mark 6. Mix the pasta sauce and paprika together and divide between the pastry bases, spreading it out almost to the edges. Bake in the preheated oven for 10–12 minutes until the pastry is puffed around the edges and pale golden in colour.

5. Remove from the oven and arrange the asparagus on top, leaving space for an egg in the middle of each pastry.

6. Crack an egg into a cup and slide into the space created. Repeat with the remaining eggs, then return the pastries to the oven for 8 minutes, or until the eggs are just set.

Potato Latkes

Serve these little pancakes on their own, or as a side to your Christmas Day brunch. They are delicious with soured cream spooned over the top.

SERVES 8   PREP 10 MINS   COOK 15–20 MINS

1 kg/2 lb 4 oz floury potatoes
1 onion
25 g/1 oz plain flour
1 egg, beaten
2 tbsp sunflower oil, for frying
salt and pepper (optional)
soured cream, to serve

1. Finely grate the potatoes and onion. Put them into a sieve and press out as much liquid as possible, then spread out on a clean tea towel. Roll up and twist the tea towel to remove any remaining moisture.

2. Place the grated vegetables in a bowl and stir in the flour. Stir in the egg and season with salt and pepper, if using.

3. Heat the oil in a frying pan until medium–hot. Drop large spoons of the mixture into the pan, pressing with a spatula to flatten, and fry in batches, turning once, for 8–10 minutes until the latkes are golden brown and cooked through.

4. Drain the latkes on kitchen paper and keep warm while you cook the remaining mixture. Serve hot with some soured cream.

Eggs Baked in Tomatoes

Eggs and tomatoes are a lovely combination – full-flavoured beef tomatoes make great nests for the eggs and their zesty cheese topping.

SERVES 4 — PREP 10 MINS — COOK 20 MINS

4 large beef tomatoes

4 eggs

2 tbsp chopped fresh oregano

4 tbsp freshly grated Parmesan cheese

1 garlic clove, halved

4 slices country bread

2 tbsp olive oil

salt and pepper (optional)

1. Preheat the oven to 220°C/425°F/Gas Mark 7. Cut a slice from the top of each tomato and scoop out the seeds and pulp. Place the tomatoes in a baking dish or tin.

2. Break an egg into each tomato, then sprinkle with oregano, and salt and pepper, if using. Sprinkle with the cheese and bake in the preheated oven for about 20 minutes, or until the eggs are just set, with runny yolks.

3. Meanwhile, rub the garlic over the bread, place on a baking sheet and drizzle with oil. Bake in the oven for 5–6 minutes, or until golden.

4. Put each tomato on a slice of bread and serve immediately.

❄ Tip ❄

KEEP AN EYE ON THE EGGS TO MAKE SURE THAT THEY DON'T OVERCOOK – THESE ARE DELICIOUS WHILE THE YOLKS ARE STILL A LITTLE RUNNY.

1

2

3

49

Pain au Chocolat Cinnamon Rolls

This is the ultimate French pâtisserie-style breakfast pastry.
Use a really good-quality dark chocolate for the best results.

SERVES 12   PREP 10 MINS, PLUS CHILLING AND COOLING   COOK 30–35 MINS

100 g/3½ oz plain chocolate, broken into pieces

320 g/11 oz ready-rolled puff pastry

25 g/1 oz butter, melted

2 tbsp caster sugar

1½ tsp ground cinnamon

1. Put the chocolate into a heatproof bowl set over a saucepan of gently simmering water and heat until melted. Remove from the heat, stir until smooth, then leave to cool for 15 minutes, stirring occasionally.

2. Unroll the pastry and place on a board. Generously brush with some of the melted butter. Leave to stand for 10 minutes, then spread the cooled chocolate all over the buttered pastry. Mix the caster sugar and cinnamon together and scatter over the chocolate.

3. Roll up the pastry, Swiss roll-style, from one long side, then brush all over with more of the melted butter. Chill in the refrigerator for 15 minutes. Preheat the oven to 220°C/425°F/Gas Mark 7. Use the remaining butter to grease a 12-hole muffin tin.

4. Using a serrated knife, slice the pastry roll into 12 even-sized rounds. Place the rounds cut-side up in the prepared tin.

5. Bake in the preheated oven for 15–20 minutes, or until risen and golden brown. Leave to cool in the tin for 5 minutes, then transfer to a wire rack. Serve warm or cold.

Festive Starters

* * * * * *

Chestnut & Pancetta Soup

Chestnuts have a real taste of winter and the delicious mix of smoky pancetta, vegetables, creamy chestnuts and rosemary makes a filling soup.

SERVES 6   *PREP 15 MINS*   *COOK 45–50 MINS*

3 tbsp olive oil

175 g/6 oz pancetta, cut into strips

2 onions, finely chopped

2 carrots, finely chopped

2 celery sticks, finely chopped

350 g/12 oz dried chestnuts, soaked overnight

2 garlic cloves, finely chopped

1 tbsp finely chopped fresh rosemary

1 litre/1¾ pints chicken stock

salt and pepper (optional)

1 tbsp extra virgin olive oil, for drizzling

1. Heat the olive oil in a large saucepan, add the pancetta and cook over a medium heat, stirring frequently, for 2–3 minutes, until starting to brown.

2. Add the onions, carrots and celery and cook, stirring frequently, for 10 minutes, or until light golden and soft.

3. Drain the chestnuts, add to the pan with the garlic and rosemary and stir well. Pour in the stock, bring to a simmer and cook, uncovered, for 30–35 minutes until the chestnuts are beginning to soften and break down.

4. Season to taste with salt and pepper, if using. Ladle the soup into warmed bowls, drizzle with extra virgin olive oil and serve immediately.

Tip

THIS IS A GREAT STANDBY RECIPE FOR CHRISTMAS ENTERTAINING. IT CAN BE PREPARED UP TO 2 DAYS BEFORE YOU NEED TO SERVE IT – JUST TRANSFER TO A BOWL, COVER WITH CLINGFILM AND CHILL IN THE FRIDGE UNTIL NEEDED.

1

2

3

Gravadlax

This is a wonderful alternative to ready-prepared smoked salmon. It takes a bit of time, but the delicious result is worth it for a festive occasion.

SERVES 8–12   PREP 10 MINS, PLUS CHILLING   COOK NONE

2 salmon fillets, skin on, about 450 g/1 lb each

6 tbsp roughly chopped fresh dill

115 g/4 oz sea salt

50 g/1¾ oz sugar

1 tbsp roughly crushed white peppercorns

buttered brown bread, to serve

lemon wedges and fresh dill sprigs, to garnish

1. Rinse the salmon fillets under cold running water and dry with kitchen paper. Put one fillet, skin-side down, in a non-metallic dish.

2. Mix the dill, sea salt, sugar and peppercorns together in a small bowl. Spread this mixture over the fillet in the dish and put the second fillet, skin-side up, on top. Put a plate, the same size as the fish, on top and weigh down with three or four food cans.

3. Chill in the refrigerator for 2 days, turning the fish about every 12 hours and basting with any juices that come out of the fish.

4. Remove the salmon from the brine and thinly slice, without slicing the skin, as you would smoked salmon. Cut the buttered bread into triangles. Garnish the salmon with lemon wedges and dill sprigs and serve.

56

Classic Melon, Parma Ham & Pecorino Salad

This classic salad makes a light and refreshing starter that won't fill you up too much before the Christmas main course.

SERVES 4	PREP 10 MINS	COOK NONE

400 g/14 oz watermelon flesh, thinly sliced

400 g/14 oz honeydew melon flesh, thinly sliced

400 g/14 oz canteloupe melon flesh, thinly sliced

140 g/5 oz sliced Parma ham

25 g/1 oz pecorino cheese shavings

25 g/1 oz fresh basil

DRESSING

4 tbsp light olive oil

4 tbsp aged sherry vinegar

salt and pepper (optional)

1. Arrange the watermelon, honeydew melon and canteloupe melon slices on a large serving platter.

2. Tear any large Parma ham slices in half, then fold them all over and around the melon.

3. To make the dressing, put the oil and vinegar in a jar, season well with salt and pepper, if using, screw on the lid and shake well. Drizzle over the melon and ham.

4. Sprinkle over the cheese and basil and serve immediately.

Blue Cheese & Herb Pâté

Vegetarian guests will be delighted with this meat-free version of a classic Christmas Day starter. Serve with plenty of granary toast.

SERVES 4   PREP 15 MINS, PLUS CHILLING   COOK 5 MINS

150 g/5½ oz vegetarian
low-fat soft cheese

350 g/12 oz fromage frais

115 g/4 oz vegetarian blue
cheese, crumbled

55 g/2 oz dried cranberries,
finely chopped

1 tbsp each chopped fresh
parsley, snipped fresh
chives, chopped fresh dill
and chopped fresh tarragon

85 g/3 oz butter

2 tbsp chopped walnuts

granary toast, to serve

1. Beat the soft cheese to loosen, then gradually beat in the fromage frais until smooth. Add the blue cheese, cranberries and herbs and stir together. Spoon the mixture into four 150-ml/5-fl oz ramekins and carefully smooth the tops.

2. Clarify the butter by gently heating it in a small saucepan until melted. Skim any foam off the surface and discard.

3. Carefully pour the clear yellow top layer into a small jug, discarding the milky liquid left in the pan.

4. Pour a little of the clarified butter over the top of each ramekin and sprinkle with the walnuts. Chill for at least 30 minutes until firm, then serve with toast.

Chicken Liver Pâté

This is a really rich pâté, so serve it sparingly if it's the starter for the big Christmas meal. Its creaminess is complemented by the crisp Melba toast.

SERVES 4–6   PREP 20 MINS, PLUS CHILLING   COOK 10 MINS

200 g/7 oz butter

225 g/8 oz trimmed chicken livers, thawed if frozen

2 tbsp Marsala

1½ tsp chopped fresh sage

1 garlic clove, roughly chopped

150 ml/5 fl oz double cream

salt and pepper (optional)

fresh sage leaves, to garnish

Melba toast, to serve

1. Melt 40 g/1½ oz of the butter in a large, heavy-based frying pan. Add the chicken livers and cook over a medium heat for 4 minutes on each side. They should be brown on the outside but still pink in the centre. Transfer to a food processor and process until finely chopped.

2. Add the Marsala to the pan and stir, scraping up any sediment with a wooden spoon, then add to the food processor with the chopped sage, garlic and 100 g/3½ oz of the remaining butter. Process until smooth. Add the cream, season to taste with salt and pepper, if using, and process until thoroughly combined and smooth. Spoon the pâté into a dish or individual ramekins, smooth the surface and leave to cool completely.

3. Melt the remaining butter in a small saucepan, then spoon it over the surface of the pâté, leaving any sediment in the pan. Leave to cool, then cover and chill in the refrigerator. Garnish with sage and serve with Melba toast.

Mixed Antipasto Meat Platter

This very useful prepare-ahead starter can be refrigerated for a couple of hours, but don't drizzle over the oil until you're just ready to serve.

SERVES 4	*PREP 20 MINS*	*COOK NONE*

1 cantaloupe melon

55 g/2 oz Italian salami, thinly sliced

8 slices prosciutto

8 slices bresaola

8 slices mortadella

4 plum tomatoes, thinly sliced

4 fresh figs, halved

115 g/4 oz black olives, stoned

2 tbsp shredded fresh basil leaves

4 tbsp extra virgin olive oil

pepper (optional)

1 tbsp extra virgin olive oil, for drizzling

1. Cut the melon in half, scoop out and discard the seeds, then cut the flesh into 8 wedges. Arrange the wedges on one half of a large serving platter.

2. Arrange the salami, prosciutto, bresaola and mortadella in loose folds on the other half of the platter. Arrange the tomato slices and fig halves on the platter.

3. Scatter the olives over the antipasto. Sprinkle the basil over the tomatoes and drizzle with olive oil. Season to taste with pepper, then drizzle with extra virgin olive oil and serve immediately.

❄ Variation ❄

IF YOU CAN'T FIND FRESH FIGS, YOU COULD USE BOTTLED ARTICHOKE HEARTS IN OLIVE OIL INSTEAD. MAKE SURE YOU BUY A GOOD-QUALITY BRAND, OTHERWISE YOU MAY END UP WITH WOODY PIECES.

Baked Oregano Lobster

This is the perfect starter when you really want to push the boat out.
Once you've prepared the lobster it's very simple to put together.

SERVES 4	PREP 30 MINS	COOK 30 MINS

4 frozen lobster tails, about 175 g/6 oz each, thawed and patted dry

4 tbsp olive oil

1 large shallot, very finely chopped

2 garlic cloves, very finely chopped

6 tbsp fine dry breadcrumbs

2 tsp dried oregano

finely grated rind of 2 lemons

1 tbsp very finely chopped fresh flat-leaf parsley

1 tbsp olive oil, for drizzling

salt and pepper (optional)

1. Preheat the oven to 180°C/350°F/Gas Mark 4. Put a lobster tail on a board, shell down. Use scissors to cut lengthways through the shell without cutting through the tail fan. Do not crush the shell. Use a small knife to cut the tail meat in half lengthways without cutting through the shell. Cut away the cartilage on top of the shell. Use the tip of a knife to cut out the black intestinal vein. Repeat with the remaining tails. Cover and chill until required.

2. Heat the oil in a small frying pan. Add the shallot and fry for 1–2 minutes, until golden. Add the garlic and stir for a further 1 minute, or until the shallot is soft. Stir in the breadcrumbs, oregano, lemon rind and parsley and season with salt and pepper, if using.

3. Very lightly season inside the split tails with salt and pepper, if using, then place the tails in a deep roasting tin, using balls of foil to wedge them upright, if necessary. Divide the oregano mixture between them, lightly pressing it into the splits and covering half the tails. Drizzle with oil. Add enough boiling water to come halfway up the sides of the tails. Bake in the preheated oven for 20 minutes, until the flesh at the thickest part of the tails is white. Remove from the oven and serve immediately.

Garlic-stuffed Mushrooms

Pine nuts give these stuffed mushrooms a really crunchy texture, and dried apricots and feta cheese provide a tasty flavour combination.

SERVES 4 ·········· **PREP 15 MINS** ·········· **COOK 10–12 MINS**

4 large field mushrooms

4 sprays olive oil

2–3 garlic cloves, crushed

2 shallots

25 g/1 oz fresh wholemeal breadcrumbs

8 fresh basil sprigs

25 g/1 oz ready-to-eat dried apricots, chopped

1 tbsp pine nuts

55 g/2 oz feta cheese

pepper (optional)

fresh basil sprigs, to garnish

1. Preheat the oven to 180°C/350°F/Gas Mark 4. Remove the stalks from the mushrooms and set aside. Spray the bases of the mushrooms with the oil and place cap-side down in a roasting tin.

2. Put the mushroom stalks in a food processor with the garlic, shallots and breadcrumbs. Place the basil sprigs in the food processor with the apricots, pine nuts and cheese. Add pepper to taste, if using.

3. Process for 1–2 minutes until the mixture has a stuffing consistency, then divide between the mushroom caps.

4. Bake in the preheated oven for 10–12 minutes, or until the mushrooms are tender and the stuffing is crisp on the top. Serve garnished with basil sprigs.

Leek & Goat's Cheese Tartlets

Serve these delicious, easy-to-prepare tartlets with a rocket salad as a sit-down starter, or on their own as part of a buffet meal.

| SERVES 6 | PREP 15 MINS | COOK 20 MINS |

375 g/13 oz (1 rectangular sheet, 35 x 23 cm/14 x 9 inches) ready-rolled puff pastry

40 g/1½ oz butter

350 g/12 oz baby leeks, thickly sliced diagonally

1 tbsp chopped fresh oregano

125 g/4½ oz goat's cheese, sliced or crumbled

1 tbsp milk, for brushing

salt and pepper (optional)

1. Preheat the oven to 220°C/425°F/Gas Mark 7. Cut the pastry into six 12-cm/4½-inch squares.

2. Place the pastry squares on a baking sheet and use the tip of a sharp knife to score each one about 1-cm/½-inch from the edge all around.

3. Melt the butter in a frying pan, add the leeks and fry gently, stirring frequently, for 4–5 minutes until soft. Add the oregano, season with salt and pepper, if using, and divide the leek mixture between the pastry squares, placing it inside the scored lines.

4. Top each tartlet with cheese and brush the pastry with milk. Bake in the preheated oven for 12–15 minutes until risen and golden brown. Serve warm.

67

Baked Figs with Gorgonzola

Made with baby figs, just melting Gorgonzola, delicate wild flower honey and crunchy wholegrain toast, this starter is quite heavenly.

SERVES 4   *PREP 15 MINS*   *COOK 10 MINS*

1 mixed-grain demi-baguette, cut into 8 x 2-cm/¾-inch thick slices (total weight 100 g/3½ oz)

8 small fresh figs

55 g/2 oz Gorgonzola cheese, rind removed, cut into 8 squares

4 tsp honey

1. Preheat the oven to 180°C/350°F/Gas Mark 4. Lightly toast the bread on both sides, then transfer to a small baking sheet.

2. Cut a cross in the top of each fig, lightly press a cube of cheese into each one, then place a fig on top of each slice of toast. Bake in the preheated oven for 5–6 minutes, until the figs are hot and the cheese is just melting.

3. Transfer to a plate. Drizzle with honey and serve immediately.

> *Tip* ALTHOUGH GORGONZOLA IS RENOWNED IN ITALY AS THE TRADITIONAL CULINARY COMPANION FOR SWEET AND JUICY FIGS, YOU CAN USE ANY BLUE CHEESE FOR THIS DISH, EVEN STILTON, IF YOU WANT TO GIVE IT A REAL TOUCH OF THE TRADITIONAL CHRISTMAS.

The Main Event

* * * * * *

Traditional Roast Chicken

If you don't have a big crowd for Christmas dinner, a large chicken, cooked and served in the same way, is a good alternative to turkey.

SERVES 6	PREP 20 MINS	COOK 1 HR 45 MINS

1 x 2.25-kg/5-lb free-range chicken

55 g/2 oz butter

2 tbsp chopped fresh lemon thyme

1 lemon, quartered

125 ml/4 fl oz white wine

salt and pepper (optional)

fresh thyme sprigs, to garnish

1. Preheat the oven to 220°C/425°F/Gas Mark 7. Make sure the chicken is clean, wiping it inside and out with kitchen paper, and place in a roasting tin. Put the butter into a bowl and soften with a fork, then mix in the chopped thyme and season with salt and pepper, if using. Butter the chicken all over with the herb butter, inside and out, and place the lemon quarters inside the body cavity. Pour the wine over the chicken.

2. Roast in the centre of the preheated oven for 20 minutes. Reduce the oven temperature to 190°C/375°F/Gas Mark 5 and roast for a further 1¼ hours, basting frequently. Cover with foil if the skin begins to brown too much. If the tin dries out, add a little more wine or water.

3. Test that the chicken is cooked by piercing the thickest part of the leg with a sharp knife or skewer and making sure the juices run clear. Remove from the oven. Transfer the chicken to a warmed serving plate, cover loosely with foil and leave to rest for 10 minutes before carving. Place the roasting tin on the top of the stove and bubble the pan juices gently over a low heat until they have reduced and are thick and glossy. Season with salt and pepper, if using. Serve the chicken with the pan juices and garnish with thyme sprigs.

Prime Rib of Beef au Jus

Prime rib of beef is just right for a special meal and is a good option for those who prefer red meat to white for their Christmas feast.

SERVES 8   PREP 10 MINS, PLUS STANDING   COOK 1 HR 40 MINS–2 HRS 25 MINS

2.7 kg/6 lb rib of beef

55 g/2 oz butter, softened

1½ tsp sea salt flakes

1 tbsp pepper

2 tbsp flour

1 litre/1¾ pints beef stock

freshly cooked vegetables and roast potatoes, to serve

1. Place the beef bone-side down in a deep-sided roasting tin. Rub the entire surface of the meat with butter, and coat evenly with the salt and pepper.

2. Leave the beef to reach room temperature for 1 hour. Preheat the oven to 230°C/450°F/Gas Mark 8. Place the beef in the preheated oven and roast, uncovered, for 20 minutes to sear the outside of the meat.

3. Reduce the oven temperature to 165°C/325°F/Gas Mark 3 and roast for 15 minutes per 450 g/1 lb of meat for medium rare (plus or minus 15 minutes for well done and rare respectively). Transfer the meat to a large platter and cover with foil. Leave to rest for 30 minutes before serving.

4. Meanwhile, pour off all but 2 tablespoons of the fat from the tin and place the tin over a medium heat. Add the flour and simmer, stirring with a wooden spoon for 1 minute until a thick paste forms. Pour in a ladleful of stock and bring to the boil, then beat into the paste, scraping all the caramelized drippings from the base of the tin until smooth. Repeat with the remaining stock, a ladleful at a time.

5. Simmer for 10 minutes until reduced and slightly thickened. Strain the sauce and keep warm.

6. Cut the beef free from the bone and carve thinly. Serve the jus alongside the carved beef, accompanied by vegetables and roast potatoes.

Roast Venison with Brandy Sauce

Saddle of venison is a delicious and seasonal choice for the festive meal, and the rich and creamy brandy sauce complements it perfectly.

SERVES 6   PREP 10 MINS   COOK 1 HR 55 MINS

6 tbsp vegetable oil

1.7 kg/3 lb 12 oz saddle of fresh venison, trimmed

salt and pepper (optional)

freshly cooked vegetables, to serve

BRANDY SAUCE

1 tbsp plain flour

4 tbsp vegetable stock

175 ml/6 fl oz brandy

100 ml/3½ fl oz double cream

1. Preheat the oven to 180°C/350°F/Gas Mark 4. Heat half the oil in a frying pan over a high heat.

2. Season the venison with salt and pepper, if using, then add to the pan and cook until lightly browned all over. Pour the remaining oil into a roasting tin. Add the venison, cover with foil and roast in the preheated oven, basting occasionally, for 1½ hours, or until cooked through. Remove from the oven and transfer to a warmed serving platter. Cover with foil and set aside.

3. To make the sauce, place the roasting tin on the hob over a medium heat, add the flour and cook for 1 minute. Pour in the stock and heat, stirring to loosen the sediment from the base of the tin. Gradually stir in the brandy and bring to the boil, then reduce the heat and simmer, stirring, for 10–15 minutes until the sauce has thickened a little. Remove from the heat and stir in the cream.

4. Serve the venison with the brandy sauce and a selection of freshly cooked vegetables.

Duck with Madeira & Blueberry Sauce

Duck breasts are a delicious main course for a small group. The Madeira and blueberry sauce is a wonderfully fresh accompaniment.

4 duck breasts, skin on

4 garlic cloves, chopped

grated rind and juice of 1 orange

1 tbsp chopped fresh parsley

salt and pepper (optional)

new potatoes and a selection of green vegetables, to serve

MADEIRA & BLUEBERRY SAUCE

150 g/5½ oz blueberries

275 ml/9 fl oz Madeira

1 tbsp redcurrant jelly

1. Use a sharp knife to make several shallow diagonal cuts in each duck breast. Put the duck in a glass bowl with the garlic, orange rind and juice and parsley. Season with salt and pepper, if using, and stir well. Turn the duck in the mixture until thoroughly coated. Cover the bowl with clingfilm and transfer to the refrigerator to marinate for at least 1 hour.

2. Heat a dry, non-stick frying pan over a medium heat. Add the duck breasts and cook for 4 minutes, then turn them over and cook for a further 4 minutes, or to taste. Remove from the heat, cover and leave to stand for 5 minutes.

3. Halfway through the cooking time, make the sauce. Put the blueberries, Madeira and redcurrant jelly into a separate saucepan. Bring to the boil. Reduce the heat and simmer for 10 minutes, then remove from the heat.

4. Slice the duck breasts and transfer to warmed serving plates. Serve with the sauce poured over and accompanied by new potatoes and green vegetables.

Festive Beef Wellington

This truly magnificent dish is worthy of centrepiece status at the festive meal – to do it justice, buy the very best-quality beef you can.

SERVES 4   PREP 30 MINS   COOK 1 HOUR 10 MINS

750 g/1 lb 10 oz thick beef fillet

2 tbsp butter

2 tbsp vegetable oil

1 garlic clove, chopped

1 onion, chopped

175 g/6 oz chestnut mushrooms, thinly sliced

1 tbsp chopped fresh sage

350 g/12 oz ready-made puff pastry, thawed if frozen

1 egg, beaten

salt and pepper (optional)

1. Preheat the oven to 220°C/425°F/Gas Mark 7. Put the beef in a roasting tin, spread with the butter and season to taste with salt and pepper, if using. Roast in the preheated oven for 30 minutes, then remove from the oven. Do not switch off the oven.

2. Meanwhile, heat the oil in a saucepan over a medium heat. Add the garlic and onion and cook, stirring, for 3 minutes. Stir in salt and pepper to taste, if using, the mushrooms and the sage and cook, stirring frequently, for 5 minutes. Remove from the heat.

3. Roll out the pastry into a rectangle large enough to enclose the beef, then place the beef in the centre and spread the mushroom mixture over it. Bring the long sides of the pastry together over the beef and seal with beaten egg. Tuck the short ends over, trimming away the excess pastry, and seal. Place on a baking sheet seam-side down and make two slits in the top. Decorate with pastry shapes made from the trimmings and brush with the beaten egg. Bake for 40 minutes. Remove from the oven, cut into thick slices and serve.

> *Tip*   YOU CAN SUBSTITUTE THE MORE USUAL MUSHROOM MIXTURE WITH A DELICIOUS ROASTED GARLIC PASTE. SIMPLY ROAST A WHOLE BULB OF GARLIC IN A HOT OVEN FOR 10 MINUTES, THEN MIX THE FLESH WITH SOME OLIVE OIL, FRESH CHOPPED THYME AND ROSEMARY, THEN SPREAD IT OVER THE BEEF.

Roast Pork Loin

Only the best will do at Christmas and this joint is superb. Rich moist meat is served with a crisp and crunchy crackling.

SERVES 6   PREP 25 MINS, PLUS RESTING   COOK 2 HRS 10 MINS

1.8 kg/4 lb flat piece
pork loin, backbone removed
and rind scored

2½ tsp salt

¼ tsp pepper

3 garlic cloves, crushed

2 tbsp chopped fresh rosemary

4 fresh rosemary sprigs

225 ml/8 fl oz dry
white wine

fresh rosemary sprigs,
to garnish

cooked seasonal vegetables,
to serve

1. Preheat the oven to 230°C/450°F/Gas Mark 8. Put the pork on a work surface, skin-side down. Make small slits in the meat all over the surface. Season with ½ teaspoon of the salt and the pepper. Rub the garlic all over the meat surface and sprinkle with the chopped rosemary.

2. Roll up the loin and secure the rosemary sprigs on the outside with fine string. Make sure that the joint is securely tied. Season the rind with the remaining salt to give a good crackling.

3. Transfer the meat to a roasting tin and roast in the preheated oven for 20 minutes, or until the fat has started to run. Reduce the oven temperature to 190°C/375°F/Gas Mark 5 and pour half the wine over the meat. Roast for a further 1 hour 40 minutes, basting the meat occasionally with the pan juices.

4. Remove the meat from the oven and leave to rest in a warm place for 15 minutes before carving. Remove the string and the rosemary before cutting into thick slices.

5. Pour off all but 1 tablespoon of the fat from the roasting tin. Add the remaining wine to the juices in the tin and bring to the boil, scraping up and stirring in any sediment from the base of the tin. Spoon over the meat and serve immediately with fresh vegetables, garnished with extra sprigs of rosemary.

Glazed Gammon

Gammon can be served as an accompaniment to the Christmas turkey, although this delicious joint deserves recognition in its own right.

| SERVES 8 | PREP 20 MINS | COOK 4 HRS 20 MINS |

4 kg/9 lb gammon
1 apple, cored and chopped
1 onion, chopped
300 ml/10 fl oz cider
6 black peppercorns
1 bouquet garni
1 bay leaf
50 cloves
4 tbsp demerara sugar

1. Put the gammon into a large saucepan and add enough cold water to cover. Bring to the boil and skim off any foam that rises to the surface. Reduce the heat and simmer for 30 minutes.

2. Drain the gammon and return to the pan. Add the apple, onion, cider, peppercorns, bouquet garni, bay leaf and a few of the cloves. Pour in enough fresh water to cover and bring back to the boil. Cover and simmer for 3 hours 20 minutes.

3. Preheat the oven to 200°C/400°F/Gas Mark 6. Take the pan off the heat and set aside to cool slightly. Remove the gammon from the cooking liquid and, while it is still warm, loosen the rind with a sharp knife, then peel it off and discard.

4. Score the fat into diamond shapes and stud with the remaining cloves. Place the gammon on a rack in a roasting tin and sprinkle with the sugar. Roast in the preheated oven, basting occasionally with the cooking liquid, for 20 minutes. Serve hot or cold.

Poached Salmon

A whole poached salmon makes an impressive and very special main course on Christmas Day. Serve with lemon and fresh vegetables.

SERVES 6	PREP 20 MINS	COOK 6–8 MINS, PLUS STANDING

1 whole salmon (head on), about 2.7 kg/6 lb–3.6 kg/ 8 lb prepared weight

3 tbsp salt

3 bay leaves

10 black peppercorns

1 onion, peeled and sliced

1 lemon, sliced

lemon wedges, to serve

1. Wipe the salmon thoroughly inside and out with kitchen paper, then use the back of a cook's knife to remove any scales that might still be on the skin. Remove the fins with a pair of scissors and trim the tail. Some people prefer to cut off the head but it is traditionally served with it on.

2. Place the salmon on the two-handled rack that comes with a fish kettle, then place it in the kettle. Fill the kettle with enough cold water to cover the salmon adequately. Sprinkle over the salt, bay leaves and peppercorns and scatter in the onion and lemon slices.

3. Place the kettle over a low heat, over two burners, and bring just to the boil very slowly.

4. Cover and simmer very gently. Simmer for 6–8 minutes and leave to stand in the hot water for 15 minutes before removing. Serve with lemon wedges for squeezing over.

Roast Monkfish with Boulangère Potatoes

Delicious firm-fleshed monkish is served here with melt-in-the-mouth Boulangère potatoes. Add crisp salad leaves for a well-rounded plate.

SERVES 4   PREP 20 MINS   COOK 55 MINS–1 HR 10 MINS

40 g/1½ oz butter, melted

700 g/1 lb 9 oz floury potatoes, peeled and very thinly sliced

1 onion, very thinly sliced

1 tbsp roughly chopped fresh thyme

200 ml/7 fl oz vegetable stock

4 skinless monkfish fillets, about 200 g/7 oz each

4 tbsp olive oil

finely pared rind of 1 lemon

8 tbsp chopped fresh flat-leaf parsley

1 garlic clove, crushed

salt and pepper (optional)

1. Preheat the oven to 200°C/400°F/Gas Mark 6. Brush a shallow ovenproof dish with a little of the melted butter. Layer the potatoes, onion and thyme in the dish, seasoning well between the layers with salt and pepper, if using, and finishing with a layer of potatoes.

2. Pour in enough of the stock to come halfway up the potatoes and drizzle the remaining melted butter over the top. Bake in the centre of the preheated oven for 40–50 minutes, pressing the potatoes into the stock once or twice with the back of a spatula until tender and brown on top.

3. Season the monkfish with salt and pepper, if using. Mix together the oil, lemon rind, parsley and garlic and rub all over the monkfish. Sear the monkfish in a smoking hot frying pan or on a griddle pan for 1 minute on each side, or until browned. Transfer the monkfish to a roasting tin, spaced well apart, and roast on the top shelf of the oven for the final 12–15 minutes of the cooking time, until just cooked through. Serve immediately with the potatoes.

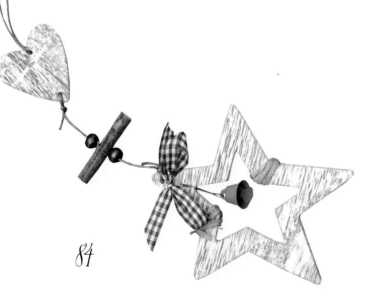

84

Mixed Nut Roast

This lusciously rich nut roast is a good vegetarian option for an indulgent Christmas dinner and it cooks much more quickly than a turkey or goose!

SERVES 4   PREP 15 MINS   COOK 35 MINS

10 g/¼ oz butter, for greasing

2 tbsp butter

2 garlic cloves, chopped

1 large onion, chopped

50 g/1¾ oz pine nuts, toasted

75 g/2¾ oz hazelnuts, toasted

50 g/1¾ oz ground walnuts

50 g/1¾ oz ground cashew nuts

100 g/3½ oz wholemeal breadcrumbs

1 egg, lightly beaten

2 tbsp chopped fresh thyme

275 ml/9 fl oz vegetable stock

salt and pepper (optional)

fresh thyme sprigs, to garnish

CRANBERRY & RED WINE SAUCE

175 g/6 oz fresh cranberries

100 g/3½ oz caster sugar

300 ml/10 fl oz red wine

1 cinnamon stick

1. Preheat the oven to 180°C/350°F/Gas Mark 4. Grease a 450-g/1-lb loaf tin and line it with greaseproof paper.

2. Melt the butter in a saucepan over a medium heat. Add the garlic and onion and cook, stirring, for about 3 minutes. Remove the pan from the heat.

3. Grind the pine nuts and hazelnuts in a mortar with a pestle. Stir into the pan with the walnuts and cashew nuts and add the breadcrumbs, egg, thyme, stock and seasoning, if using.

4. Spoon the mixture into the prepared tin and level the surface. Cook in the centre of the preheated oven for 30 minutes or until cooked through and golden and a skewer inserted into the centre of the loaf comes out clean.

5. Halfway through the cooking time, make the sauce. Put the cranberries, sugar, wine and cinnamon into a saucepan over a medium heat and bring to the boil. Reduce the heat and simmer, stirring occasionally, for 15 minutes.

6. Remove the nut roast from the oven and turn out onto a serving platter. Garnish with thyme sprigs and serve.

1

4

5

Roast Butternut Squash

Butternut squash has a lovely flavour – stuffed with beans, mushrooms and courgettes, it makes a substantial vegetarian or vegan main course.

SERVES 4   PREP 40 MINS, PLUS STANDING   COOK 1 HR 10 MINS

1 butternut squash, about 450 g/1 lb

1 onion, chopped

2–3 garlic cloves, crushed

4 small tomatoes, chopped

85 g/3 oz chestnut mushrooms, chopped

85 g/3 oz canned butter beans, drained, rinsed and roughly chopped

1 courgette, about 115 g/4 oz, trimmed and grated

2 tbsp chopped fresh oregano

2 tbsp tomato purée

300 ml/10 fl oz water

4 spring onions, trimmed and chopped

1 tbsp vegetarian Worcestershire sauce

pepper (optional)

1. Preheat the oven to 190°C/375°F/Gas Mark 5. Prick the squash all over with a metal skewer then roast in the preheated oven for 40 minutes, or until tender. Remove from the oven and leave to stand until cool enough to handle. Do not switch off the oven.

2. Cut the squash in half, scoop out and discard the seeds, then scoop out some of the flesh, making hollows in both halves. Chop the scooped-out flesh and put in a bowl. Place the two squash halves side by side in a large roasting tin.

3. Add the onion, garlic, tomatoes and mushrooms to the squash flesh in the bowl. Add the beans, courgette, half the oregano and pepper, if using, and mix well together. Spoon the filling into the two halves of the squash, packing it down as firmly as possible.

4. Mix the tomato purée with the water, spring onions and Worcestershire sauce in a small bowl and pour around the squash.

5. Cover loosely with a large sheet of foil and bake for 30 minutes, or until piping hot. Serve in warmed bowls, garnished with the remaining oregano.

1

3

4

89

Roast Beetroot Parcels with Polenta

Beetroot with horseradish is an amazing combination; the lovely sweet earthiness of the beetroot complemented by the bite of the horseradish.

SERVES 4	PREP 20 MINS, PLUS COOLING	COOK 2 HRS

2 tbsp olive oil, for greasing and tossing

8 small beetroots, peeled and halved

4 fresh thyme sprigs

4 tbsp grated fresh horseradish, or grated horseradish from a jar

125 g/4½ oz unsalted butter

salt and pepper (optional)

rocket leaves, to serve

POLENTA

900 ml/1½ pints water

175 g/6 oz quick-cook polenta

1 tsp salt

1. To make the polenta, bring the water to the boil in a large saucepan. Slowly add the polenta and salt, stirring constantly. Simmer, stirring frequently, for 30–40 minutes, until the mixture comes away from the side of the pan.

2. Grease a small roasting tin. Tip the polenta into the tin, level the surface and leave to cool.

3. Preheat the oven to 190°C/375°F/Gas Mark 5. Toss the beetroots with enough oil to coat.

4. Place 4 beetroot halves and a thyme sprig on a square of thick foil. Season with salt and pepper, if using. Wrap in a loose parcel, sealing the edges. Repeat with the remaining beetroot halves, to make four parcels in total. Roast in the preheated oven for 1 hour, or until just tender.

5. Meanwhile, mash the horseradish with the butter, and a little salt and pepper, if using. Roll into a log using a piece of clingfilm and chill in the refrigerator.

6. Preheat the grill to high. Slice the polenta into four neat rectangles. Spread out in a grill pan, brush with oil and cook under a hot grill for 5 minutes. Turn and grill for a further 3 minutes until crisp.

7. Arrange the polenta on serving plates. Place the beetroot and a slice of horseradish butter on top and serve with rocket.

Superb Sides
& Sauces

* * * * *

Perfect Roast Potatoes

With a crisp, golden crust and steaming hot and fluffy white flesh, roast potatoes are the ideal accompaniment to a traditional Christmas dinner.

SERVES 8 **PREP 25 MINS** **COOK 1 HR 25 MINS**

---

70 g/2½ oz goose fat

1 tsp coarse sea salt

1 kg/2 lb 4 oz even-sized floury potatoes

fresh rosemary sprigs, to garnish

1. Preheat the oven to 230°C/450°F/Gas Mark 8. Put the fat in a large roasting tin, sprinkle generously with the salt and place in the preheated oven.

2. Meanwhile, bring a large saucepan of water to the boil, add the potatoes, bring back to the boil and cook for 8–10 minutes until parboiled. Drain well and, if the potatoes are large, cut them in half. Return the potatoes to the empty pan and shake vigorously to roughen them on the outside.

3. Arrange the potatoes in a single layer in the hot fat and roast in the preheated oven for 45 minutes. If they look as if they are beginning to char around the edges, reduce the oven temperature to 200°C/400°F/Gas Mark 6. Turn the potatoes over and roast for a further 30 minutes until crisp. Garnish with rosemary sprigs and serve immediately.

❄ Tip ❄

TOSS THE PARBOILED POTATOES IN A LITTLE ENGLISH MUSTARD POWDER TO GIVE AN EXTRA GOLDEN CRUST. IF YOU CAN'T GET GOOSE FAT, USE THE SAME QUANTITY OF DUCK FAT OR 5 TABLESPOONS OF OLIVE OIL INSTEAD.

Mashed Sweet Potatoes

This tasty mash is a delicious accompaniment to any roast meat, and its lovely warm colour will enhance the Christmas dining table.

SERVES 4	PREP 10 MINS	COOK 25 MINS, PLUS STANDING

70 g/2½ oz butter, softened

2 tbsp chopped fresh parsley

900 g/2 lb sweet potatoes, scrubbed

1. Reserving 25 g/1 oz, put the butter into a bowl with the parsley and beat together. Turn out onto a square of foil or clingfilm, shape into a block and transfer to the refrigerator to chill until required.

2. Cut the sweet potatoes into even-sized chunks. Bring a large saucepan of water to the boil, add the sweet potatoes, bring back to the boil and cook, covered, for 15–20 minutes until tender.

3. Drain the potatoes well, then cover the pan with a clean tea towel and leave to stand for 2 minutes. Remove the skins and mash with a potato masher until fluffy.

4. Add the reserved butter to the potatoes and stir in evenly. Spoon the mash into a serving dish and serve hot, topped with chunks of parsley butter.

1

3

3

Sticky Carrots with Whisky & Ginger Glaze

Sweet carrots are given added zing with a spicy whisky glaze, making them a worthy accompaniment to the Christmas roast meats.

SERVES 2–3	PREP 15 MINS	COOK 20 MINS

1 tsp sugar

½ tsp pepper

good pinch of sea salt flakes

4 tbsp groundnut oil

3 tbsp lightly salted butter

4 large carrots, sliced diagonally into 1-cm/ ½-inch rounds

2-cm/¾-inch piece fresh ginger, cut into batons

2 tbsp whisky

125 ml/4 fl oz chicken stock

1. Mix the sugar, pepper and salt together in a bowl and set aside until needed.

2. Heat the oil with half the butter in a large frying pan. Add the carrots in a single layer and sprinkle with the sugar mixture. Cook over a medium–high heat for 3 minutes, then start turning the slices with tongs and reduce the heat if necessary. When brown on both sides and starting to blacken at the edges, transfer to a plate.

3. Wipe out the pan with kitchen paper. Add the ginger and cook over a medium–high heat for 1–2 minutes, until golden. Add to the carrots.

4. Add the remaining butter, the whisky and stock. Bring to the boil, then reduce the heat and simmer for 3 minutes or until syrupy. Return the carrots and ginger to the pan and swirl with the syrup for 1 minute. Serve immediately.

Pecan-glazed Brussels Sprouts

Perfectly cooked nutty-flavoured Brussels sprouts are given some extra festive crunch with the addition of golden toasted pecan nuts.

SERVES 6	PREP 15 MINS	COOK 35 MINS

650 g/1 lb 7 oz Brussels sprouts

125 ml/4 fl oz water

55 g/2 oz unsalted butter

70 g/2½ oz soft light brown sugar

3 tbsp soy sauce

¼ tsp salt

60 g/2¼ oz finely chopped pecan nuts, toasted

1. Cut off the stem ends of the sprouts and slash the base of each sprout with a shallow 'X'. Bring the water to the boil in a large saucepan; add the sprouts, cover, then reduce the heat and simmer for 8–10 minutes, or until the sprouts are slightly softened, then drain and set aside.

2. Melt the butter in a frying pan and stir in the sugar, soy sauce and salt. Bring to the boil, stirring constantly. Add the nuts, reduce the heat and simmer, uncovered, for 5 minutes, stirring occasionally. Add the sprouts and cook over a medium heat for 5 minutes. Stir well before serving.

❄ *Variation* ❄

FOR A MORE TRADITIONAL FINISH TO THIS DISH, YOU COULD SUBSTITUTE THE PECAN NUTS WITH CHOPPED OR FLAKED BLANCHED ALMONDS.

Cranberry Sauce

Succulent and zingy cranberry sauce is the perfect accompaniment to roast turkey – and you can use any leftovers in the turkey sandwiches!

SERVES 8　　　　*PREP 20 MINS*　　　　*COOK 5 MINS*

thinly pared rind and juice of
1 lemon

thinly pared rind and juice of
1 orange

350 g/12 oz cranberries,
thawed if frozen

140 g/5 oz caster sugar

2 tbsp arrowroot, mixed with
3 tbsp cold water

1. Place the lemon rind and orange rind in a heavy-based saucepan. Add the cranberries, lemon juice, orange juice and sugar to the pan and cook over a medium heat, stirring occasionally, for 5 minutes, or until the berries begin to burst.

2. Strain the juice into a clean saucepan and reserve the cranberries. Stir the arrowroot mixture into the juice, then bring to the boil, stirring constantly, until smooth and thick. Remove from the heat and stir in the reserved cranberries.

3. Transfer the cranberry sauce to a bowl and leave to cool, then cover with clingfilm and chill in the refrigerator until ready to use.

Garlic Mushrooms with Chestnuts

That all-time favourite, garlic mushrooms, is given a festive twist with the addition of chestnuts, cream and a splash of white wine.

SERVES 4   PREP 15 MINS   COOK 15 MINS

55 g/2 oz butter

4 garlic cloves, chopped

200 g/7 oz button mushrooms, sliced

200 g/7 oz chestnut mushrooms, sliced

4 tbsp dry white wine

100 ml/3½ fl oz double cream

300 g/10½ oz canned whole chestnuts, drained

100 g/3½ oz chanterelle mushrooms, sliced

salt and pepper (optional)

chopped fresh parsley, to garnish

1. Melt the butter in a large saucepan over a medium heat. Add the garlic and cook, stirring, for 3 minutes, until soft. Add the button mushrooms and chestnut mushrooms and cook for 3 minutes.

2. Stir in the wine and cream and season with salt and pepper, if using. Cook for 2 minutes, stirring, then add the chestnuts and the chanterelle mushrooms. Cook for a further 2 minutes, stirring, then remove from the heat and transfer to a warmed serving dish. Garnish with chopped fresh parsley and serve.

Rich Onion Gravy

The secret to well-flavoured gravy is to use a really good-quality stock – home-made if possible.

SERVES 8   PREP 15 MINS   COOK 1 HR 25 MINS

2 tbsp sunflower oil

450 g/1 lb onions, thinly sliced

2 garlic cloves, crushed

1 tbsp sugar

25 g/1 oz plain flour

150 ml/5 fl oz red wine

600 ml/1 pint boiling beef stock

2 tsp Dijon mustard

pinch of gravy browning (optional)

salt and pepper (optional)

1. Heat the oil in a large, heavy-based saucepan. Add the onions, garlic and sugar and fry over a low heat for 30 minutes, stirring occasionally, until very soft and light golden in colour.

2. Stir in the flour and cook for 1 minute. Add the wine and bring to the boil, then simmer and beat until the mixture is smooth. Add 150 ml/5 fl oz of the stock and bring back to the boil. Simmer and beat again to mix thoroughly.

3. Stir in the remaining stock, mustard and gravy browning, if using. Bring back to the boil and season with salt and pepper, if using.

4. Simmer for 20 minutes and serve immediately.

Mango & Macadamia Stuffing

Much of the appeal of the Christmas turkey is the stuffing, for which there are many variations. The exotic flavours make this one a bit different.

SERVES 4–6   PREP 10 MINS   COOK 30 MINS

---

10 g/¼ oz butter, for greasing

25 g/1 oz butter

1 small onion, finely chopped

1 celery stick, diced

175 g/6 oz fresh white breadcrumbs

1 egg, beaten

1 tbsp Dijon mustard

1 small mango, peeled, stoned and diced

85 g/3 oz macadamia nuts, chopped

salt and pepper (optional)

1. Preheat the oven to 200°C/400°F/Gas Mark 6. Grease a 750-ml/1¼-pint ovenproof dish.

2. Melt the butter in a saucepan, add the onion and fry, stirring, for 3–4 minutes until soft. Add the celery and cook for a further 2 minutes.

3. Remove from the heat and stir in the breadcrumbs, egg and mustard. Add the mango and nuts, then season to taste with salt and pepper, if using.

4. Spread the mixture in the prepared dish and bake in the preheated oven for 20–25 minutes until golden and bubbling. Serve hot.

> *Tip* YOU CAN USE SOME OF THE MIXTURE TO STUFF THE NECK END OF THE BIRD BEFORE ROASTING, AND BAKE THE REMAINDER OF THE STUFFING ACCORDING TO THE RECIPE, OR YOU CAN ROLL IT INTO WALNUT-SIZED BALLS AND BAKE IT IN THE OVEN FOR 15–20 MINUTES.

Divine Desserts

* * * * * *

Cheesecake with Caramel Pecan Nuts

This delicious baked cheesecake, with its lovely caramelized pecan nut decoration, is a dessert worthy of gracing the Christmas table.

SERVES 6–8   PREP 25 MINS   COOK 1 HR 20 MINS–1 HR 30 MINS

BASE

50 g/1¾ oz pecan nuts

150 g/5½ oz digestive biscuits, broken into pieces

50 g/1¾ oz butter, melted

FILLING

400 g/14 oz cream cheese

200 g/7 oz curd cheese

125 g/4½ oz unrefined caster sugar

3 large eggs

3 large egg yolks

200 ml/7 fl oz double cream

TOPPING

10 g/¼ oz butter, for greasing

225 g/8 oz unrefined caster sugar

5 tbsp water

70 g/2½ oz pecan nuts

1. Preheat the oven to 160°C/325°F/Gas Mark 3. To make the base, put the nuts in a food processor and process briefly, then add the broken biscuits and pulse again until crumbs form. Tip into a bowl and stir in the melted butter until well combined. Press into the base of a 20-cm/8-inch round springform cake tin. Bake in the preheated oven for 10 minutes, then remove from the oven and leave to cool.

2. To make the filling, beat together the cream cheese, curd cheese and sugar in a large bowl. Beat in the eggs and egg yolks, one at a time, until smooth. Finally, stir in the cream. Spoon over the prepared base. Bake in the preheated oven for 1 hour, then test – the cheesecake should be cooked but with a slight 'wobble' in the centre. Return to the oven for a further 10 minutes if necessary. Remove from the oven and leave to cool in the tin.

3. To make the topping, grease a piece of foil with butter and lay it flat. Put the sugar and water in a saucepan and heat gently, stirring, until the sugar has dissolved. Bring to a simmer, swirling the saucepan rather than stirring, and cook until the syrup begins to darken, then add the pecan nuts. Transfer each nut to the greased foil and leave to harden. When you are ready to serve, unmould the cheesecake onto a serving plate and arrange the caramel pecan nuts on top.

1

2

3

Apple Pie

This classic dessert is perfect to round off Christmas dinner. Add more cinnamon to the filling if you're feeling extra festive!

SERVES 6–8 PREP 40 MINS, PLUS CHILLING COOK 50 MINS

175 g/6 oz plain flour

pinch of salt

85 g/3 oz butter, cut into pieces

85 g/3 oz lard, cut into small pieces

about 1–2 tbsp water

1 egg, beaten, for glazing

10 g/¼ oz soft light brown sugar, for sprinkling

FILLING

750 g–1 kg/1 lb 10 oz–2 lb 4 oz cooking apples, peeled, cored and sliced

125 g/4½ oz soft light brown sugar

½–1 tsp ground cinnamon

1. Sift the flour and salt into a mixing bowl. Add the butter and lard and rub in with your fingertips until the mixture resembles fine breadcrumbs. Add enough cold water to mix to a firm dough. Wrap in clingfilm and chill for 30 minutes.

2. Preheat the oven to 220°C/425°F/Gas Mark 7. Thinly roll out almost two thirds of the pastry and use to line a deep 23-cm/9-inch pie dish.

3. To make the filling, mix the apples with the sugar and cinnamon and pack into the pastry case.

4. Roll out the remaining pastry to make a lid. Dampen the edges of the pie rim with water and position the lid, pressing the edges firmly together. Trim and crimp the edges. Use the pastry trimmings to cut out leaves or other shapes. Dampen and attach to the top of the pie. Glaze the pie with beaten egg, make one or two slits in the top and place the pie on a baking sheet.

5. Bake in the preheated oven for 20 minutes, then reduce the temperature to 180°C/350°F/Gas Mark 4 and bake for a further 30 minutes, or until the pastry is a light golden brown. Sprinkle with sugar and serve hot or cold.

114

115

Prosecco
& Lemon Sorbet

This deliciously light and refreshing dessert is lovely after a heavy meal –
or you could serve it as a palate cleanser between courses.

SERVES 4   PREP 10 MINS, PLUS COOLING AND FREEZING   COOK 5 MINS

140 g/5 oz caster sugar

100 ml/3½ fl oz water

finely grated rind and juice
of 1 lemon

350 ml/12 fl oz prosecco

fresh mint sprigs, to decorate

1. Put the sugar, water and lemon rind into a medium-sized saucepan over a low heat and heat, stirring constantly, until the sugar is dissolved.

2. Bring to the boil, then boil for 1 minute until slightly reduced. Leave to cool, then strain through a sieve.

3. Add the lemon juice and prosecco to the lemon syrup and stir to combine, then pour into an ice-cream machine and churn following the manufacturer's instructions. Alternatively, pour into a container to freeze and whisk once an hour until completely frozen.

4. Remove the sorbet from the freezer about 15 minutes before serving, then scoop into serving dishes. Decorate with mint sprigs and serve.

Cranberry Amaretti Creams

All the lovely flavours of Christmas – ginger, cinnamon and tart, juicy cranberries – come together in this luscious and creamy cold dessert.

SERVES 10   PREP 15 MINS, PLUS COOLING AND CHILLING   COOK 10 MINS

85 g/3 oz granulated sugar

2 tsp cornflour

large pinch of ground cinnamon

large pinch of ground ginger

125 ml/4 fl oz water

200 g/7 oz frozen cranberries

150 g/5½ oz full-fat soft cheese

3 tbsp caster sugar

200 ml/7 fl oz double cream

4 tsp orange juice

55 g/2 oz amaretti biscuits, crushed

1. Put the granulated sugar, cornflour, cinnamon and ginger into a heavy-based saucepan, then gradually add the water, stirring, until smooth. Add the cranberries and cook for 5–8 minutes, stirring occasionally, until they are soft and the mixture has thickened. Cover and leave to cool.

2. Put the cheese and caster sugar into a mixing bowl and stir, then gradually whisk in the cream until smooth. Stir in the orange juice and then the biscuit crumbs. Spoon the mixture into a disposable paper or polythene piping bag. Spoon the cranberry mixture into a separate disposable piping bag. Snip off the tips.

3. Pipe the amaretti cream into ten shot glasses until they are one-quarter full. Pipe over half the cranberry mixture, then repeat the layers. Cover and chill.

Pear & Ginger Bundt Cakes

Bundt cakes have become a traditional Christmas offering – these perfect miniature versions, with their luscious whisky glaze, are irresistible.

SERVES 12   PREP 20 MINS   COOK 35–40 MINS

10 g/¼ oz butter, for greasing

10 g/¼ oz flour, for dusting

250 g/9 oz pears, peeled, cored and cubed

1 tbsp dark muscovado sugar

125 g/4½ oz butter, softened

175 g/6 oz caster sugar

2 eggs, beaten

100 ml/3½ fl oz soured cream

175 g/6 oz plain flour, sifted

1 tsp baking powder

1 tsp ground ginger

pinch of salt

4 tbsp finely chopped crystallized ginger

2 tsp vanilla extract

GLAZE

2 tbsp whisky

50 g/1¾ oz dark muscovado sugar

1. Preheat the oven to 180°C/350°F/Gas Mark 4. Grease a 12-hole mini Bundt tin and lightly dust with flour, shaking out any excess.

2. Place the pears in a small saucepan with a splash of cold water and the muscovado sugar. Cook over a low heat for 3–4 minutes, until the pears are soft, but not mushy. Drain through a sieve, reserving the cooking juices, and leave to cool.

3. Place the butter and caster sugar in a mixing bowl and beat until light and fluffy. Gradually beat in the eggs, adding a spoonful of the flour if the mixture curdles. Stir in the soured cream.

4. Mix the flour with the baking powder, ground ginger, salt and 2 tablespoons of the crystallized ginger, then gently fold into the mixture with the vanilla extract and the pears.

5. Spoon the mixture into the prepared tin and bake in the preheated oven for 25–30 minutes until risen and golden. Leave to cool in the tin for a few minutes, then transfer to a wire rack to cool completely.

6. To make the glaze, place the reserved cooking juices in a small saucepan with the whisky and sugar, bring to the boil and boil hard for 2–3 minutes until slightly reduced and thickened. Spoon over the tops of the cakes and scatter over the remaining crystallized ginger.

Cranberry Apple Meringues

Apples cooked until tender with zesty dried cranberries, then covered with a soft meringue topping – it all adds up to a delicious dessert.

SERVES 4	PREP 10 MINS	COOK 25–30 MINS

500 g/1 lb 2 oz cooking apples

1 tbsp apple juice

175 g/6 oz caster sugar

100 g/3½ oz dried cranberries

2 egg whites

1. Preheat the oven to 200°C/400°F/Gas Mark 6. Peel, core and chop the apples, place in a saucepan and sprinkle with the apple juice.

2. Add 70 g/2½ oz of the sugar and the cranberries, stir and heat gently until boiling. Cover the pan, reduce the heat and simmer gently, stirring occasionally, for 8–10 minutes until the fruit is just tender.

3. Divide the fruit between four 350-ml/12-fl oz ovenproof dishes and place on a baking sheet.

4. Put the egg whites into a grease-free bowl and whisk until they hold soft peaks. Gradually whisk in the remaining sugar until the mixture holds stiff peaks.

5. Spoon the meringue on top of the fruit, swirling with a knife. Bake in the preheated oven for 10–12 minutes until the meringue is lightly browned. Serve warm.

❄ Tip ❄

THIS IS A GOOD DINNER PARTY DESSERT BECAUSE IT'S SO EASY TO PREPARE AHEAD. JUST COOK THE APPLE MIXTURE AND SET ASIDE UNTIL NEEDED, THEN REHEAT AND PROCEED WITH THE RECIPE FROM STEP 3.

Poached Pears

Pears poached in Marsala make a very elegant dessert — they are an excellent standby as they can be prepared well in advance.

SERVES 6   PREP 20 MINS, PLUS CHILLING AND COOLING   COOK 50 MINS–1 HR 5 MINS

6 dessert pears, peeled but left whole with stalks attached

500 ml/17 fl oz Marsala

125 ml/4 fl oz water

1 tbsp soft brown sugar

1 piece of lemon rind or mandarin rind

1 vanilla pod

350 ml/12 fl oz double cream

1 tbsp icing sugar

1. Put the pears in a large saucepan with the Marsala, water, brown sugar and lemon rind and gently bring to the boil, stirring to make sure that the sugar has dissolved. Reduce the heat, cover and simmer for 30 minutes until the pears are tender. Leave the pears to cool in the liquid, then remove from the liquid, cover and chill in the refrigerator.

2. Discard the lemon rind and simmer the liquid for 15–20 minutes, or until syrupy. Leave to cool.

3. Cut a thin sliver of flesh from the base of each pear so that they will stand upright. Slit open the vanilla pod and scrape out the seeds into a bowl. Whisk together the cream, vanilla seeds and icing sugar in a bowl until thick. Put each pear on a dessert plate and pour over a little syrup. Serve with the vanilla cream.

Variation YOU COULD ADD A FEW PIECES OF CHOPPED STEM GINGER TO THE SYRUP WHEN IT HAS COOLED, AND SERVE THE PEARS WITH SOME STEM GINGER OR CINNAMON ICE CREAM INSTEAD OF THE VANILLA CREAM.

122

Mango & Ginger Roulade

Mango and ginger are brought together in a delicious combination for this luscious dessert, which is perfect for entertaining.

SERVES 6   PREP 30 MINS   COOK 15–20 MINS

1 tbsp oil, for oiling

10 g/¼ oz golden caster sugar, for sprinkling

150 g/5½ oz plain white flour

1½ tsp baking powder

175 g/6 oz butter, softened

175 g/6 oz golden caster sugar

3 eggs, beaten

1 tsp vanilla extract

2 tbsp orange juice

1 large ripe mango

3 tbsp chopped glacé ginger

5 tbsp crème fraîche

1. Preheat the oven to 180°C/350°F/Gas Mark 4. Oil a 23 x 33-cm/9 x 13-inch Swiss roll tin and line with baking paper, leaving an overhang of 1 cm/½ inch above the rim. Lay a sheet of baking paper on the work surface and sprinkle with caster sugar.

2. Sift the flour and baking powder into a large bowl and add the butter, sugar, eggs and vanilla extract. Beat well until smooth, then beat in the orange juice. Spoon the mixture into the prepared tin and smooth into the corners with a palette knife. Bake in the preheated oven for 15–20 minutes, or until risen, firm and golden brown.

3. Meanwhile, peel and stone the mango and cut into chunks. Reserve a few pieces for decoration and finely chop the remainder. Transfer to a small bowl and stir in 2 tablespoons of the glacé ginger.

4. Turn out the sponge onto the prepared paper and spread with the mango mixture. Firmly roll up the sponge from one short side to enclose the filling, keeping the paper around the outside to hold it in place. Carefully transfer to a wire rack to cool, removing the paper when firm.

5. When cold, top with spoonfuls of crème fraîche and decorate with the reserved mango and the remaining glacé ginger.

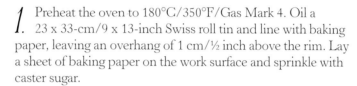

Chocolate Mousse

This simplest of desserts is one of the most satisfying. To get the best flavour, make sure you use the best plain chocolate.

SERVES 4–6	PREP 10 MINS, PLUS CHILLING	COOK 6–10 MINS

280 g/10 oz plain chocolate, broken into small pieces

1½ tbsp unsalted butter

1 tbsp brandy

4 eggs, separated

55 g/2 oz plain chocolate, broken into small pieces, to serve

1. Place the chocolate and butter in a heatproof bowl set over a saucepan of gently simmering water, and heat, stirring, until smooth. Remove from the heat, stir in the brandy, and leave to cool slightly. Add the egg yolks and beat until smooth.

2. In a separate bowl, whisk the egg whites until they hold stiff peaks, then fold into the chocolate mixture. Spoon into small serving bowls or glasses and level the surfaces. Transfer to the refrigerator and chill for 4 hours, or until set.

3. Take the mousse out of the refrigerator and serve, sprinkled with chopped chocolate pieces.

1

2

2

Rich Chocolate Pies

Chocolate and cream, baked together in a rich and delicious pie — what could be better as a dessert during the indulgent festive season?

SERVES 8   PREP 20 MINS, PLUS CHILLING   COOK 35 MINS

PASTRY

225 g/8 oz plain flour
115 g/4 oz butter, diced
2 tbsp icing sugar
1 egg yolk
2–3 tbsp cold water
10 g/¼ oz flour, for dusting

FILLING

250 g/9 oz plain chocolate, broken into pieces
115 g/4 oz butter
50 g/1¾ oz icing sugar
300 ml/10 fl oz double cream
grated chocolate, to decorate

1. To make the pastry, sift the flour into a large bowl. Add the butter and rub it in with your fingertips until the mixture resembles breadcrumbs. Add the icing sugar, egg yolk and enough water to form a soft dough. Wrap the dough in clingfilm and chill in the refrigerator for 15 minutes. Roll out the pastry on a lightly floured surface and use to line eight 10-cm/4-inch shallow tartlet tins. Chill for 30 minutes.

2. Preheat the oven to 200°C/400°F/Gas Mark 6. Prick the cases with a fork and line with crumpled foil. Bake in the preheated oven for 10 minutes, then remove the foil and bake for a further 5–10 minutes. Transfer to a wire rack to cool. Reduce the oven temperature to 160°C/325°F/Gas Mark 3.

3. To make the filling, place the chocolate, butter and icing sugar in a heatproof bowl set over a saucepan of gently simmering water and heat until melted. Remove from the heat and stir in 200 ml/7 fl oz of the cream. Remove the pastry cases from the tins and place on a baking sheet. Fill each case with some of the chocolate mixture. Return to the oven and bake for 5 minutes. Remove from the oven and leave to cool, then chill until required.

4. Whip the remaining cream and pipe into the centre of each tart. Decorate with grated chocolate and serve.

Yuletide Baking

* * * * *

Christmas Tree Wreath Cake

Celebrate the festive season with this delightful themed cake – with the added surprise of Christmas tree sponge running through the middle.

SERVES 16   PREP 60 MINS, PLUS CHILLING   COOK 1 HR 55 MINS, PLUS COOLING

GREEN SPONGE
10 g/¼ oz butter, for greasing

10 g/¼ oz flour, for dusting

225 g/8 oz self-raising flour

¼ tsp baking powder

225 g/8 oz butter, softened

225 g/8 oz caster sugar

4 large eggs

green food colouring paste

VANILLA SPONGE
250 g/9 oz self-raising flour

225 g/8 oz butter, softened

225 g/8 oz caster sugar

4 large eggs

1 tsp vanilla extract

TO DECORATE
525 g/1 lb 3 oz ready-made vanilla buttercream

2 tsp mixed red, white and green confetti sugar sprinkles

1 tsp silver dragées

1. Preheat the oven to 160°C/325°F/Gas Mark 3. Thoroughly grease a 2-litre/3½-pint ring cake tin, then lightly dust with flour.

2. To make the green sponge, place the self-raising flour, baking powder, butter, sugar and eggs in a large bowl and beat with a hand-held electric mixer for 1–2 minutes until smooth and creamy. Beat in enough food colouring to give the mixture a Christmas tree-green colour.

3. Spoon the mixture into the prepared tin and level the surface. Bake in the preheated oven for 45–50 minutes, or until risen, firm to the touch and a skewer inserted into the middle of the cake comes out clean. Leave to cool in the tin for 10 minutes, then turn out carefully onto a wire rack and leave to cool completely. Switch off the oven.

4. Place the cold cake on a board and use a sharp knife to cut it into 16 wedge-shaped slices. Slightly separate the slices (still maintaining the ring shape), then chill in the freezer for 30 minutes.

5. Use a Christmas tree-shaped cookie cutter to stamp out 16 Christmas tree shapes from the chilled sponge wedges. Re-form the trees into the ring shape again and return to the freezer for a further 30–40 minutes, or until very firm.

6. Meanwhile, preheat the oven to 160°C/325°F/Gas Mark 3. Clean the tin, then grease it and lightly dust with flour.

7. To make the vanilla sponge, place all the ingredients in a large bowl and beat with a hand-held electric mixer for 1–2 minutes until smooth and creamy. Spoon the mixture into a piping bag fitted with a plain nozzle.

8. Pipe three lines of mixture into the base of the prepared tin, then continue piping the mixture up the side of the tin and smooth with a palette knife.

9. Take two Christmas tree sponge cake shapes together and gently place in the vanilla mixture, pointed side down and leaning in to the centre of the tin. Repeat with the remaining slices, keeping them as close together as possible, to re-form the ring shape (upside down) inside the tin.

10. Pipe the remaining vanilla mixture around the other sides of the trees and over the tops to cover them completely. Gently level the surface.

11. Bake in the preheated oven for 45 minutes, then loosely cover the top of the cake with foil. Bake for a further 15–20 minutes, or until a skewer inserted into the cake comes out clean (make sure to place the skewer right into the cake in an area where there is more vanilla sponge). Leave to cool in the tin for 15 minutes. Run a small angled palette knife around the side of the cake, carefully turn out onto a wire rack and leave to cool completely.

12. To decorate, spread some of the buttercream in a thin layer all over the cake. Chill the cake in the refrigerator for 30 minutes. Spread the remaining buttercream all over the cake, swirling it with a palette knife. Decorate with confetti sprinkles and silver dragées.

Dark Chocolate Yule Log

This chocolate delight is the traditional French and Belgian Christmas cake – when you've sampled it, you'll see why it's so popular.

SERVES 8   PREP 45 MINS, PLUS COOLING   COOK 20 MINS

10 g/¼ oz butter, for greasing

10 g/¼ oz flour, for dusting

10 g/¼ oz caster sugar, for sprinkling

150 g/5½ oz caster sugar

4 eggs, separated

1 tsp almond extract

115 g/4 oz self-raising flour

280 g/10 oz plain chocolate, broken into squares

225 ml/8 fl oz double cream

2 tbsp rum

holly sprig, to decorate

10 g/¼ oz icing sugar, for dusting

1. Preheat the oven to 190°C/375°F/Gas Mark 5. Grease a 40 x 28-cm/16 x 11-inch Swiss roll tin, line with baking paper, then dust with flour. Sprinkle a sheet of greaseproof paper with caster sugar.

2. Reserving 2 tablespoons, put the caster sugar into a bowl with the egg yolks and whisk until thick and pale. Stir in the almond extract. Whisk the egg whites in a separate bowl until they hold soft peaks. Gradually whisk in the reserved sugar until the mixture is stiff and glossy.

3. Sift half the flour into the egg yolk mixture and fold in, then fold in one quarter of the egg white. Sift and fold in the remaining flour, followed by the remaining egg whites. Spoon the mixture into the prepared tin, spreading it evenly with a palette knife. Bake in the preheated oven for 15 minutes, until lightly golden. Turn out onto the prepared paper, then roll up and leave to cool.

4. Place the chocolate in a heatproof bowl. Bring the cream to boiling point in a small saucepan, then pour it over the chocolate and stir until the chocolate has melted. Beat until smooth and thick. Reserve about one third of the chocolate mixture and stir the rum into the remainder. Unroll the cake and spread with the chocolate and rum mixture. Re-roll and place on a large plate or silver board. Evenly spread the reserved chocolate mixture over the top and side of the cake. Mark with a fork so that the surface resembles tree bark. Just before serving, decorate with a holly sprig and sprinkle with icing sugar to resemble snow.

Festive Cupcakes

These delicately decorated, mixed fruit and orange cupcakes will take pride of place on your table.

MAKES 14	PREP 20 MINS, PLUS COOLING	COOK 15–20 MINS

115 g/4 oz mixed dried fruit

1 tsp finely grated orange rind

2 tbsp brandy or orange juice

85 g/3 oz butter, softened

85 g/3 oz light soft brown sugar

1 large egg, lightly beaten

115 g/4 oz self-raising flour

1 tsp mixed spice

1 tbsp silver dragées (cake decoration balls), to decorate

ICING

85 g/3 oz icing sugar

2 tbsp orange juice

1. Put the mixed fruit, orange rind and brandy in a small bowl. Cover and leave to soak for 1 hour.

2. Preheat the oven to 190°C/375°F/Gas Mark 5. Put 14 paper baking cases in 2 bun trays or put 14 double-layer paper cases on a baking tray.

3. Put the butter and sugar in a mixing bowl and beat together until light and fluffy. Gradually beat in the egg. Sift in the flour and mixed spice and, using a metal spoon, fold them into the mixture followed by the soaked fruit. Spoon the mixture into paper cases.

4. Bake the cupcakes in the preheated oven for 15–20 minutes or until golden brown and firm to the touch. Transfer to a cooling rack and leave to cool.

5. To make the icing, sift the icing sugar into a bowl and gradually mix in enough orange juice until the mixture is smooth and thick enough to coat the back of a wooden spoon. Using a teaspoon, drizzle the icing in a zig-zag pattern over the cupcakes. Decorate with the silver dragées. Leave to set.

Holly Cupcakes

These picture-perfect iced cupcakes are quick to make and easy to decorate and will certainly impress your guests.

MAKES 16   PREP 45 MINS, PLUS COOLING   COOK 20 MINS

125 g/4½ oz butter, softened

200 g/7 oz caster sugar

4 eggs, lightly beaten

a few drops of almond extract

150 g/5½ oz self-raising flour

175 g/6 oz ground almonds

450 g/1 lb white ready-to-roll fondant icing

10 g/¼ oz icing sugar, for dusting

55 g/2 oz green ready-to-roll fondant icing

25 g/1 oz red ready-to-roll fondant icing

1. Preheat the oven to 180°C/350°F/Gas Mark 4. Line two 8-hole muffin tins with paper cases.

2. Place the butter and caster sugar in a large bowl and beat together until light and fluffy. Gradually beat in the eggs and almond extract. Sift in the flour and, using a metal spoon, fold into the mixture with the ground almonds.

3. Spoon the mixture into the paper cases. Bake in the preheated oven for 20 minutes, or until the cupcakes are risen, golden and firm to the touch. Transfer to a wire rack and leave to cool completely.

4. Roll out the white fondant icing to a thickness of 5 mm/¼ inch on a surface lightly dusted with icing sugar. Using a 7-cm/2¾-inch plain cutter, stamp out 16 rounds, re-rolling the icing as necessary. Place a round on top of each cupcake.

5. Roll out the green fondant icing to the same thickness. Using a holly cutter, cut out 32 leaves, re-rolling the icing as necessary. Brush each leaf with a little water and place two leaves on top of each cupcake. Roll the red fondant icing to make 48 small berries and place on the leaves.

Apple & Cinnamon Bran Muffins

These delicious, gluten-free muffins are so delicious that you will want to make them all year round!

MAKES 12   PREP 15 MINS   COOK 20–25 MINS

4 tbsp vegetable oil

1 tbsp glycerine

175 g/6 oz apple purée

2 eggs

½ tsp vanilla extract

55 g/2 oz clear honey

75 ml/2½ fl oz milk

300 g/10½ oz gluten-free, wheat-free plain flour

120 g/4¼ oz gluten-free, wheat-free oat bran

70 g/2½ oz ground linseeds

1 tsp gluten-free baking powder

½ tsp gluten-free bicarbonate of soda

½ tsp xanthan gum

1 tsp cinnamon

¼ tsp mixed spice

175 g/6 oz soft light brown sugar

60 g/2¼ oz raisins

60 g/2¼ oz sultanas

1. Preheat the oven to 180°C/350°F/Gas Mark 4. Line a 12-hole muffin tin with paper cases.

2. In a large bowl, whisk together the oil, glycerine, apple purée, eggs, vanilla extract, honey and milk. In a separate bowl, mix all the remaining ingredients together then add the liquid mixture and stir well.

3. Divide the mixture between the paper cases. Bake the muffins in the preheated oven for 20–25 minutes, or until a skewer inserted into the centre of a muffin comes out clean. Remove from the oven and leave to cool on a wire rack.

> *Tip* IF YOU LIKE, YOU COULD ADD SOME CHOPPED ALMONDS, HAZELNUTS, WALNUTS, PECAN NUTS OR MACADAMIA NUTS TO THE DRY INGREDIENTS TO GIVE THE MUFFINS A LITTLE CRUNCH AND EXTRA FLAVOUR.

Christmas Macaroons

With their Christmas-flavoured filling and sparkling gold decoration, these delicious mouthfuls will certainly enhance the festivities.

MAKES 16   PREP 40 MINS. PLUS STANDING   COOK 10–15 MINS

75 g/2¾ oz ground almonds

115 g/4 oz icing sugar

1 tsp ground mixed spice

2 large egg whites

50 g/1¾ oz golden caster sugar

½ tsp freshly grated nutmeg

1 tsp gold dragées

FILLING

55 g/2 oz unsalted butter, softened

juice and finely grated rind of ½ orange

1 tsp ground mixed spice

115 g/4 oz icing sugar, sifted

25 g/1 oz glacé cherries, finely chopped

1. Place the ground almonds, icing sugar and mixed spice in the bowl of a food processor and process for 15 seconds. Sift the mixture into a bowl. Line two baking sheets with greaseproof paper.

2. Place the egg whites in a large bowl and whisk until they hold soft peaks. Gradually whisk in the caster sugar to make a firm, glossy meringue. Using a spatula, fold the almond mixture into the meringue one third at a time. When all the dry ingredients are thoroughly incorporated, continue to cut and fold the mixture until it forms a shiny batter with a thick, ribbon-like consistency.

3. Pour the mixture into a piping bag fitted with a 1-cm/½-inch plain nozzle. Pipe 32 small rounds onto the prepared baking sheets. Tap the baking sheets firmly on a work surface to remove air bubbles. Sprinkle half the macaroons with the grated nutmeg and gold dragées. Leave at room temperature for 30 minutes. Meanwhile, preheat the oven to 160°C/325°F/ Gas Mark 3.

4. Bake the macaroons in the preheated oven for 10–15 minutes. Leave to cool for 10 minutes, then carefully peel the macaroons off the paper. Transfer to a wire rack and leave to cool completely.

5. To make the filling, beat the butter in a bowl with the orange juice and rind until fluffy. Gradually beat in the mixed spice and icing sugar until smooth and creamy. Fold in the glacé cherries and use the mixture to sandwich pairs of macaroons together.

1

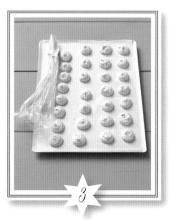

3

5

Christmas Cranberry & Orange Pies

If you're a lover of cranberry sauce, you'll be delighted with these delicious little fruit pies, filled with the taste of Christmas.

MAKES 12   *PREP 15 MINS, PLUS COOLING*   *COOK 30 MINS*

10 g/¼ oz butter, for greasing

175 g/6 oz frozen cranberries

1 tbsp cornflour

3 tbsp freshly squeezed orange juice

2 star anise

55 g/2 oz caster sugar

225 g/8 oz ready-made sweet shortcrust pastry, chilled

10 g/¼ oz plain flour, for dusting

1 tbsp milk, for brushing

10 g/¼ oz caster sugar, for sprinkling

1. Preheat the oven to 180°C/350°F/Gas Mark 4. Lightly grease a 12-hole mini muffin tin. Put the cranberries in a saucepan with the cornflour and orange juice. Add the star anise and cook over a low heat, stirring occasionally, for 5 minutes, or until the cranberries are soft. Add the sugar and cook for a further 5 minutes, then remove from the heat and leave to cool.

2. Thinly roll out the pastry on a lightly floured surface. Using a fluted cookie cutter, stamp out 12 x 6-cm/ 2½-inch rounds and gently press into the prepared tin, reserving the trimmings. Brush the top edges of the pie cases with a little milk. Remove and discard the star anise, then spoon in the filling.

3. Thinly roll out the pastry trimmings. Using a fluted pastry wheel, cut out thin strips of pastry. Arrange these over each pie in a lattice pattern, brush with milk and sprinkle with sugar. Bake in the preheated oven for 20 minutes. Leave to cool in the tin for 10 minutes, then transfer to a wire rack. Serve warm or cold.

Christmas Tree Biscuits

If you like to make your own Christmas decorations, you'll love these, but don't be surprised if they mysteriously disappear from the tree!

MAKES 12   PREP 20 MINS, PLUS CHILLING AND COOLING   COOK 10–12 MINS

150 g/5½ oz plain flour

1 tsp ground cinnamon

½ tsp freshly grated nutmeg

½ tsp ground ginger

70 g/2½ oz unsalted butter, diced

3 tbsp honey

10 g/¼ oz butter, for greasing

10 g/¼ oz plain flour, for dusting

white icing and silver dragées (optional) and narrow ribbon, to decorate

1. Sift the flour and spices into a bowl and rub in the butter until the mixture resembles breadcrumbs. Add the honey and mix well together to form a soft dough. Halve the dough, shape into balls, wrap in clingfilm and chill in the refrigerator for 30 minutes.

2. Preheat the oven to 180°C/350°F/Gas Mark 4 and lightly grease two baking sheets. Roll out one piece of dough on a floured work surface to thickness of 5 mm/¼ inch. Cut out tree shapes using a cutter. Repeat with the remaining dough.

3. Put the biscuits on the prepared baking sheets and, using a cocktail stick, make a hole through the top of each biscuit large enough to thread the ribbon through. Chill in the refrigerator for 15 minutes.

4. Bake in the preheated oven for 10–12 minutes until golden. Leave to cool on the baking sheets for 5 minutes, then transfer to a wire rack to cool completely. Decorate the trees with icing and silver dragées, or leave them plain. Thread the ribbon through the biscuits and hang them on the Christmas tree.

Rudolph Cookies

Everyone loves a Christmas-themed cookie and these reindeer ones are sure to go down well with children and adults alike!

MAKES 16   PREP 30 MINS, PLUS CHILLING AND COOLING   COOK 15–18 MINS

100 g/3½ oz unsalted butter, softened

100 g/3½ oz caster sugar

1 small egg

175 g/6 oz self-raising flour

ICING

100 g/3½ oz icing sugar

2–3 tsp cold water

TO DECORATE

small pretzels

red sweets

chocolate sprinkles

1. Place the butter in a large bowl and beat with a hand-held electric mixer until soft. Add the caster sugar, egg and flour and beat well to make a smooth dough. Wrap in clingfilm and chill in the refrigerator for 10 minutes. Line two baking sheets with baking paper.

2. Unwrap the dough and divide into 16 pieces, rolling with your hands into slightly oval balls. Place on the prepared baking sheets, spaced well apart to allow for spreading.

3. Carefully slice off the top of each pretzel with a serrated knife. Press two pretzels into the top of each cookie for antlers. Chill in the refrigerator for 10 minutes. Meanwhile, preheat the oven to 180°C/350°F/Gas Mark 4.

4. Bake in the preheated oven for 15–18 minutes until just golden. Leave to cool on the baking sheets for a few minutes, then transfer to wire racks to cool completely.

5. To make the icing, sift the icing sugar into a bowl and gradually add the water, stirring to a thick, toothpaste-like consistency. Spoon into a squeezy icing bottle.

6. Pipe a dab of icing in the centre of each cookie and press on a red sweet for the nose. Pipe two small dabs of icing for eyes and top each with a chocolate sprinkle. Leave to dry.

1

3

6

Mini Gingerbread House Cookies

Have fun decorating each of these mini gingerbread houses differently. Colour the royal icing with food colouring and use different sweets.

MAKES 16	PREP 30 MINS, PLUS CHILLING	COOK 15–20 MINS

125 g/4½ oz butter

2 tbsp golden syrup

175 g/6 oz light muscovado sugar

300 g/10½ oz self-raising flour

2 tsp ground ginger

1 large egg, beaten

ROYAL ICING

150 g/5½ oz icing sugar

2 tsp egg white powder

2 tbsp cold water

TO DECORATE

red and green sweets

1. Place the butter and golden syrup in a saucepan and heat gently, stirring, until melted. Remove the pan from the heat and stir in the sugar, until dissolved.

2. Sift the flour and ginger into a large bowl and make a well in the centre with a wooden spoon. Pour in the warm ingredients and the beaten egg and stir until a smooth dough forms. Wrap the dough in clingfilm and chill in the refrigerator for about 20 minutes or until just firm. Line two baking sheets with baking paper.

3. Unwrap the dough and place between two large sheets of baking paper. Roll out to an even thickness of 5 mm/¼ inch. Use a knife to cut the dough into 24 x 7-cm/2¾-inch squares. Cut eight of the squares in half diagonally to make 16 triangles.

4. Carefully transfer the squares to the prepared baking sheets. Place a triangle next to each square, with the long side touching one side of the square to make a roof for the house. Chill in the refrigerator for 10 minutes. Meanwhile, preheat the oven to 160°C/325°F/Gas Mark 3.

5. Bake the cookies in the preheated oven for 12–15 minutes until firm and lightly browned. Leave to cool on the baking sheets for a few minutes, then transfer to wire racks to cool completely.

6. To make the royal icing, sift the icing sugar into a large bowl and add the egg white powder and water. Stir with a spoon until smooth, then use an electric hand-held mixer to beat the icing for 3–4 minutes until it is thick, like toothpaste.

7. Spoon the royal icing into a piping bag fitted with a No.2 nozzle. Pipe a line of icing around the roof of each cookie and pipe roof tiles, if wished. Add a front door and windows. Pipe jagged lines under the roofs and on the ground for icicles and snow. Decorate with red and green sweets. Leave the icing to set.

Get in the Spirit

* * * * *

Holiday Eggnog

This sweet and creamy drink has a welcome hit of brandy and a touch of rum for that winter warming effect on a cold day.

SERVES 9	PREP 10 MINS, PLUS CHILLING	COOK 25 MINS

6 large eggs

100 g/3½ oz caster sugar, plus 2 tbsp extra

575 ml/18 fl oz single cream

575 ml/18 fl oz milk

125 ml/4 fl oz brandy

4 tbsp light rum

1 tsp vanilla extract

575 ml/18 fl oz double cream

freshly grated nutmeg, to decorate

1. Whisk the eggs with a hand-held electric mixer on medium speed until thick and lemon in colour, then gradually add the 100 g/3½ oz sugar, whisking well.

2. Put the single cream and milk into a large saucepan over a medium–low heat and heat until very hot but not boiling. Gradually add the hot milk mixture to the egg mixture, stirring with a balloon whisk. Return the mixture to the pan and cook over a medium–low heat, stirring constantly with a balloon whisk until very hot but not boiling. Remove from the heat and leave to cool. Stir in the brandy, rum and vanilla extract with a balloon whisk. Cover and chill in the refrigerator until thoroughly chilled.

3. Just before serving, whip the double cream with the remaining sugar in a large bowl until it holds soft peaks. Pour the chilled eggnog mixture into a large punch bowl. Gently fold the whipped cream into the eggnog mixture just until combined. Decorate with freshly grated nutmeg.

Mulled Ale & Mulled Wine

These classic recipes have really stood the test of time. Apart from tasting delicious, they will fill your kitchen with warm and spicy aromas.

....

MAKES 2.8L/5 PINTS | *PREP 20 MINS, PLUS STANDING* | *COOK 35 MINS*

....

MULLED ALE
2.5 litres / 4½ pints strong ale

300 ml / 10 fl oz brandy

2 tbsp caster sugar

large pinch of ground cloves

large pinch of ground ginger

MULLED WINE
5 oranges

50 cloves

thinly pared rind and juice of 4 lemons

850 ml / 1½ pints water

115 g / 4 oz caster sugar

2 cinnamon sticks

2 litres / 3½ pints red wine

150 ml / 5 fl oz brandy

1. To make the mulled ale, put all the ingredients in a heavy-based saucepan and heat gently, stirring, until the sugar has dissolved. Continue to heat so that it is simmering but not boiling. Remove the saucepan from the heat and serve the ale immediately in heatproof glasses.

2. To make the mulled wine, prick the skins of 3 of the oranges all over with a fork and stud with the cloves, then set aside. Thinly pare the rind and squeeze the juice from the remaining oranges.

3. Put the orange rind and juice, lemon rind and juice, water, sugar and cinnamon in a heavy-based saucepan and bring to the boil over a medium heat, stirring occasionally, until the sugar has dissolved. Boil for 2 minutes without stirring, then remove from the heat, stir once and leave to stand for 10 minutes. Strain the liquid into a heatproof jug.

4. Pour the wine into a separate saucepan and add the strained spiced juices, the brandy and the clove-studded oranges. Simmer gently without boiling, then remove from the heat. Strain into heatproof glasses and serve immediately.

Kir Royale

A truly luxurious drink for a festive drinks party. The addition of a little brandy gives this innocent-tasting cocktail a kick.

SERVES 1   *PREP 2 MINS*   *COOK NONE*

few drops crème de cassis, or to taste
½ measure brandy
champagne, chilled
fresh mint spring, to decorate

1. Put the cassis into the bottom of a champagne flute.

2. Add the brandy. Top up with champagne.

3. Decorate with the mint sprig and serve immediately.

❄ Variation ❄

OMIT THE CRÈME DE CASSIS, PLACE A SUGAR CUBE AND A DASH OF ANGOSTURA BITTERS IN THE BOTTOM OF THE CHAMPAGNE FLUTE AND POUR OVER THE BRANDY AND CHAMPAGNE FOR A STRAIGHT CHAMPAGNE COCKTAIL.

Buck's Fizz

The perfect cocktail for an extra-special Christmas brunch. Bright and fresh-tasting, this classic drink will have you celebrating in style.

SERVES 1	PREP 2 MINS	COOK NONE

2 measures chilled fresh orange juice

2 measures champagne, chilled

1. Half fill a chilled flute with orange juice.

2. Gently pour in the chilled champagne.

3. Serve immediately.

❄ Variation ❄

MAKE A JUG OF BUCK'S FIZZ UP SO THAT YOUR GUESTS CAN SERVE THEMSELVES, LEAVING YOU FREE TO PREPARE THE REST OF THE FOOD. YOU COULD SUBSTITUTE CAVA OR EVEN PROSECCO FOR CHAMPAGNE IF YOU LIKE.

Hot Brandy Chocolate

*The natural affinity between brandy and chocolate is well demonstrated
here. Whipped cream adds that extra touch of Christmas indulgence.*

SERVES 4	PREP 5 MINS	COOK 20 MINS

1 litre/1¾ pints milk

115 g/4 oz plain chocolate,
broken into pieces

2 tbsp sugar

4 measures brandy

6 tbsp whipped cream

freshly grated nutmeg,
for sprinkling

1. Heat the milk in a small saucepan to just below boiling.

2. Add the chocolate and sugar and stir over a low heat until the chocolate has melted.

3. Pour into four warmed heatproof glasses, then carefully pour 1 measure of the brandy over the back of a spoon into each glass.

4. Add the whipped cream and sprinkle over the grated nutmeg. Serve immediately.

Midnight's Kiss

Drink it at midnight, or at any other time – this flute of clear sapphire loveliness will add glamour and sparkle to any party.

SERVES 1	PREP 5 MINS	COOK NONE

sugar

wedge of lemon

½ measure vodka

2 tsp blue curaçao

cracked ice

sparkling wine

1. Spread the sugar on a plate. Run a wedge of lemon around the rim of a chilled champagne flute to moisten it, and then dip the glass in the sugar.

2. Add the vodka and curaçao to a shaker filled with ice.

3. Shake well, strain into the glass and top up with sparkling wine. Serve immediately.

Tip

YOU CAN USE ANY SUGAR FOR RIMMING THE GLASS — OR BUY GOLD SUGAR FROM A SPECIALIST SUPPLIER TO INCREASE THE GLAMOUR FACTOR OF THIS COCKTAIL.

Stuffed Olives

Olives are a traditional standby canapé, and it's always useful to have a jar to hand – the delicious stuffings in these make them really delectable.

SERVES 6   PREP 20 MINS   COOK NONE

4 tbsp Spanish extra virgin olive oil

1 tbsp sherry vinegar, or to taste

2 tbsp very finely chopped parsley

finely grated rind of ½ orange

18 large stoned black olives

18 large stoned green olives

12 anchovy fillets in oil, drained

½ grilled red pepper in oil, drained and cut into 12 small pieces

12 blanched almonds

1. Whisk together the oil, vinegar, parsley and orange rind in a small serving bowl, adding extra vinegar to taste. Set aside until needed.

2. Make a lengthways slit in 12 of the black olives and 12 of the green olives without cutting all the way through.

3. Roll up the anchovy fillets and gently press them into the cavities of 6 of the slit green olives and 6 of the slit black olives.

4. Use the pieces of red pepper to stuff the remaining slit olives. Slip a blanched almond into the centre of each of the remaining olives.

5. Add all the olives to the bowl of dressing and stir gently. Serve with wooden cocktail sticks for spearing the olives.

Stuffed Mini Peppers

Filled with oozing cheese, these tasty little morsels are perfect for serving as canapés for a seasonal drinks party.

SERVES 12	PREP 30–35 MINS	COOK 15 MINS

1 tbsp olive oil, for oiling

70 g/2½ oz full-fat cream cheese

2 garlic cloves, finely chopped

2 tsp finely chopped fresh rosemary

1 tbsp finely chopped fresh basil

1 tbsp finely chopped fresh parsley

15 g/½ oz finely grated Parmesan cheese

150 g/5½ oz cooked chicken breast, finely chopped

3 spring onions, finely chopped

12 mixed baby peppers, about 350 g/12 oz total weight

salt and pepper (optional)

1. Preheat the oven to 190°C/375°F/Gas Mark 5. Lightly brush a large baking sheet with oil.

2. Put the cream cheese, garlic, rosemary, basil and parsley in a bowl, then add the Parmesan cheese and stir together with a metal spoon.

3. Mix in the chicken and spring onions, then season with a little salt and pepper, if using.

4. Slit each pepper from the tip up to the stalk, leaving the stalk in place, then make a small cut just to the side, so that you can get a teaspoon into the centre of the pepper to scoop out the seeds.

5. Fill each pepper with some of the chicken mixture, then place on the prepared baking sheet. Cook in the preheated oven for 15 minutes, or until the peppers are soft and light brown in patches.

6. Leave to cool slightly on the baking sheet, then transfer to a serving plate. Serve warm or cold. These are best eaten on the day they are made and should be kept in the refrigerator if serving cold.

Mini Turkey Pies with Cranberry Relish

These mini turkey pies will carry the traditional taste of Christmas through to any evening get together after the big day.

SERVES 12   PREP 20 MINS, PLUS COOLING   COOK 33–35 MINS

300 g/10½ oz ready-made shortcrust pastry, chilled

10 g/¼ oz plain flour, for dusting

1 egg yolk mixed with 1 tbsp water, for glazing

300 g/10½ oz minced turkey

4 spring onions, finely chopped

2 garlic cloves, finely chopped

leaves from 4 fresh thyme sprigs

1 tsp ground allspice

2 egg yolks

salt and cayenne pepper (optional)

CRANBERRY RELISH

1 tbsp olive oil

1 red onion, thinly sliced

85 g/3 oz frozen cranberries

3 tbsp cranberry sauce

4 tbsp ruby port or red wine

1. Preheat the oven to 180°C/350°F/Gas Mark 4. Line a 12-hole muffin tin with squares of non-stick baking paper.

2. Thinly roll out the pastry on a lightly floured surface. Using a 12.5-cm/5-inch plain round cutter, stamp out 12 rounds. Press these gently into the prepared tin, so the pastry stands just above the top of the tin in soft pleats, rerolling the trimmings as needed. Brush the top edges of the pie cases with a little of the egg glaze.

3. Put the turkey, onions, garlic and thyme leaves into a mixing bowl. Sprinkle over the allspice and a little salt and cayenne pepper, if using, then stir in the egg yolks until well mixed. Spoon the filling into the pie cases and press the tops flat with the back of a teaspoon.

4. Bake in the preheated oven for 30 minutes, or until the pastry is golden and the filling is cooked through. Leave to cool in the tins for 5 minutes, then loosen with a round-bladed knife and transfer to a wire rack until needed.

5. Meanwhile, to make the relish, heat the oil in a frying pan, add the onion and cook until just beginning to soften. Add the remaining ingredients and cook for 3–4 minutes, or until the cranberries are soft. Spoon over the top of the baked pies and serve.

Blinis with Prawns & Wasabi Cream

These unusual and delicious little canapés couldn't be more dainty, and could certainly grace the most elegant of cocktail parties.

SERVES 6 — **PREP 30 MINS, PLUS CHILLING AND STANDING** — **COOK 10–15 MINS**

350 g/12 oz plain flour

125 g/4½ oz buckwheat flour

2 tsp easy-blend dried yeast

600 ml/1 pint milk, warmed

6 eggs, separated

3 tbsp unsalted butter, melted

5 tbsp soured cream

50 g/1¾ oz clarified butter

WASABI CREAM

200 ml/7 fl oz soured cream
or crème fraîche

½ tsp wasabi paste,
or to taste

salt (optional)

TO SERVE

300 g/10½ oz cooked prawns,
peeled and deveined

50 g/1¾ oz pickled ginger,
thinly sliced

2 tbsp fresh coriander leaves

1. Sift together the plain flour and buckwheat into a large bowl and stir in the yeast. Make a hollow in the centre and add the milk, then gradually beat in the flour until you have a smooth batter. Cover and chill in the refrigerator overnight.

2. Two hours before you need the blinis, remove the batter from the refrigerator and leave to stand for 1 hour 20 minutes to return to room temperature. Beat in the egg yolks, melted butter and soured cream. In a separate bowl, whisk the egg whites until stiff, then gradually fold into the batter. Cover and leave to rest for 30 minutes.

3. Meanwhile, make the wasabi cream. Mix the soured cream and wasabi paste together in a small bowl until combined. Taste and add a little more wasabi paste if you like it hotter. Season to taste with salt, if using, then cover and chill in the refrigerator.

4. To cook the blinis, heat a little of the clarified butter in a non-stick frying pan over a medium–high heat. When hot and sizzling, drop in 3–4 tablespoons of the batter, spaced well apart, and cook until puffed up and tiny bubbles appear around the edges. Flip them over and cook for a few more minutes on the other side. Remove from the pan and keep warm while you cook the remaining batter.

5. To serve, spoon a little of the wasabi cream onto a blini, add 1–2 prawns and a few slices of pickled ginger, then scatter with a few coriander leaves.

Mozzarella Crostini with Pesto & Caviar

These traditional Italian appetizers are given the festive touch when cut into the familiar symbols of a traditional Christmas.

SERVES 4	PREP 25 MINS	COOK 15 MINS

8 slices white bread, crusts removed

3 tbsp olive oil

200 g/7 oz firm mozzarella cheese, diced

6 tbsp lumpfish roe

PESTO

75 g/2¾ oz fresh basil, finely chopped

35 g/1¼ oz pine nuts, finely chopped

2 garlic cloves, finely chopped

3 tbsp olive oil

1. Preheat the oven to 180°C/350°F/Gas Mark 4. Using a sharp knife, cut the bread into fancy shapes, such as half-moons, stars and Christmas trees. Drizzle with the oil, transfer to an ovenproof dish and bake in the preheated oven for 15 minutes.

2. While the bread is baking, make the pesto. Put the basil, pine nuts and garlic in a small bowl. Pour in the oil and stir well to combine.

3. Remove the bread shapes from the oven and leave to cool. Spread a layer of pesto on all of the shapes, top each one with a piece of mozzarella cheese and some lumpfish roe and serve immediately.

Bruschetta with Broad Beans & Goat's Cheese

A wonderful summer flavour served as a vegetarian appetizer at a winter party – feta cheese is a tasty alternative to the goat's cheese.

SERVES 6	PREP 30 MINS	COOK 25 MINS

600 g/1 lb 5 oz shelled small broad beans (about 2.5 kg/5 lb 8 oz unshelled weight)

3 tbsp extra virgin olive oil

1 tbsp lemon juice

1 tbsp chopped fresh mint leaves

6 slices ciabatta

1 large garlic clove, halved

1 tsp extra virgin olive oil, for drizzling

6 tbsp soft fresh vegetarian goat's cheese

sea salt flakes and pepper (optional)

1. Bring a large saucepan of water to the boil. Add the beans, bring back to the boil and cook for 3 minutes, until just tender. Rinse under cold running water and drain. Slip off the bean skins and discard.

2. Toss the beans with the oil, lemon juice and most of the mint. Season with a little salt and pepper, if using.

3. Tip the bean mixture into a food processor. Process briefly to a chunky purée.

4. Toast the bread on both sides. While the bread is still warm, rub one side of each slice with the cut garlic clove. Drizzle with oil.

5. Cut each bread slice in half. Spread with the bean mixture, top with goat's cheese and serve immediately.

Lovely Leftovers

✳ ✳ ✳ ✳ ✳ ✳

Turkey Club Sandwiches

These sandwiches solve the perennial problem of what to do with all that leftover turkey – home-made mayonnaise is the making of them.

SERVES 6 **PREP 30 MINS** **COOK 10 MINS**

12 pancetta rashers

18 slices white bread

12 slices cooked turkey breast meat

3 plum tomatoes, sliced

6 Little Gem lettuce leaves

6 stuffed olives

salt and pepper (optional)

MAYONNAISE

2 large egg yolks

1 tsp English mustard powder

1 tsp salt

300 ml/10 fl oz groundnut oil

1 tsp white wine vinegar

1. First, make the mayonnaise. Put the egg yolks in a bowl, add the mustard powder, pepper to taste, if using and salt and beat together well. Pour the oil into a jug. Begin to whisk the egg yolks, adding just 1 drop of the oil. Make sure that this has been thoroughly absorbed before adding another drop and whisking well.

2. Continue adding the oil, 1 drop at a time, until the mixture thickens and stiffens – at this point, whisk in the vinegar and then continue to dribble in the remaining oil very slowly in a thin stream, whisking constantly, until all the oil has been used and you have a thick mayonnaise. Cover and refrigerate while you prepare the other sandwich components.

3. Grill or fry the pancetta until crisp, drain on kitchen paper and keep warm. Toast the bread until golden, then cut off the crusts. You will need three slices of toast for each sandwich. For each sandwich, spread the first piece of toast with a generous amount of mayonnaise, top with two slices of turkey, keeping the edges neat, and then top with a couple of slices of tomato. Season to taste with salt and pepper, if using. Add another slice of toast and top with two pancetta rashers and one lettuce leaf. Season to taste again, add a little more mayonnaise, then top with the final piece of toast. Push a cocktail stick through a stuffed olive, and then push this through the sandwich to hold it together.

Chicken & Dumplings

This classic dish comes together in a flash when you use leftover roast chicken, and it's just right for a warming meal on a cold day.

SERVES 4   PREP 20 MINS   COOK 35 MINS

2 tbsp olive oil

1 large onion

2 celery sticks

2 carrots

1 tbsp fresh thyme leaves

1 tsp salt

½ tsp pepper

4 tbsp butter

60 g/2¼ oz plain flour

2 tbsp milk

1.4 litres/2½ pints chicken stock

450 g/1 lb cold roast chicken

140 g/5 oz frozen peas

2 tbsp fresh parsley leaves, to garnish

DUMPLINGS

2 tbsp butter

25 g/1 oz fresh chives

250 g/9 oz plain flour

2 tsp baking powder

¾ tsp salt

225 ml/8 fl oz milk

1. Heat the oil in a large, heavy-based saucepan over a medium–high heat. Dice the onion, celery and carrots and add them to the pan. Cook, stirring, for about 3 minutes until the onion is translucent. Add the thyme, salt and pepper and cook for a further minute. Add the butter and heat until melted, then stir the flour into the butter. Cook until the butter and flour have browned. Stir in the milk and add the stock. Bring to the boil, then reduce the heat to medium and simmer for about 10 minutes. Meanwhile, shred the chicken.

2. To make the dumplings, place the butter in a microwave-safe dish. Cover the dish and cook on Low for 30 seconds, or until melted. Snip the chives. Put the flour, baking powder and salt into a bowl and stir to combine. Stir in the butter, milk and chives until just combined.

3. Stir the chicken and peas into the stew, then drop small spoonfuls of the dumpling batter on top. Cover and simmer for 12–15 minutes until the dumplings are cooked through. Meanwhile, finely chop the parsley. Ladle the stew and dumplings into warmed bowls. Garnish with parsley and serve immediately.

Turkey Soup with Rice, Mushrooms & Sage

This delicious soup makes good use of the leftover turkey and the stock you've made from the carcass, although chicken stock will do just as well.

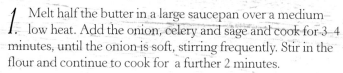

SERVES 4–5　　　*PREP 20 MINS*　　　*COOK 1 HR*

3 tbsp butter

1 onion, finely chopped

1 celery stick, finely chopped

25 large fresh sage leaves, finely chopped

4 tbsp plain flour

1.2 litres/2 pints turkey stock

100 g/3½ oz brown rice

250 g/9 oz mushrooms, sliced

200 g/7 oz cooked turkey, diced

200 ml/7 fl oz double cream

salt and pepper (optional)

sprigs of fresh sage, to garnish

freshly grated Parmesan cheese, to serve

1. Melt half the butter in a large saucepan over a medium-low heat. Add the onion, celery and sage and cook for 3–4 minutes, until the onion is soft, stirring frequently. Stir in the flour and continue to cook for a further 2 minutes.

2. Slowly add about one quarter of the stock and stir well, scraping the base of the pan to mix in the flour. Pour in the remaining stock, stirring to combine, and bring to the boil.

3. Stir in the rice and season to taste with salt and pepper, if using. Reduce the heat and simmer gently, partially covered, for about 30 minutes until the rice is just tender, stirring occasionally.

4. Meanwhile, melt the remaining butter in a large frying pan over a medium heat. Add the mushrooms and season to taste with salt and pepper, if using. Cook for about 8 minutes, until golden brown, stirring occasionally at first, then more often after they start to colour. Add the mushrooms to the soup.

5. Add the turkey to the soup and stir in the cream. Continue to simmer for about 10 minutes, until heated through. Taste and adjust the seasoning, if necessary. Ladle into warmed serving bowls, garnish with sage and serve with Parmesan cheese.

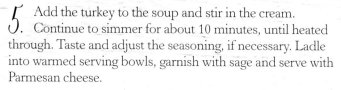

Christmas Turkey Salad

This salad provides a solution to the problem of all the little dishes of leftovers that crowd out the fridge after the Christmas meal.

SERVES 4   PREP 10 MINS   COOK NONE

125 ml/4 fl oz olive oil

4 tbsp lemon juice

3 tbsp cranberry sauce

1 tbsp grainy mustard

280 g/10 oz leftover cooked vegetables (such as carrots, green beans, broccoli)

225 g/8 oz leftover roast potatoes

300 g/10½ oz rocket

500 g/1 lb 2 oz cooked turkey, sliced

55 g/2 oz Parmesan cheese shavings

1. Whisk together the oil, lemon juice, cranberry sauce and mustard with a fork until combined.

2. Chop the cooked vegetables and roast potatoes into bite-sized pieces, place in a large bowl, add half the dressing and toss until the vegetables are coated.

3. Divide the rocket between four serving plates. Pile the vegetables on top and arrange the turkey over the vegetables. Scatter the cheese shavings over the top and serve with the remaining dressing, to taste.

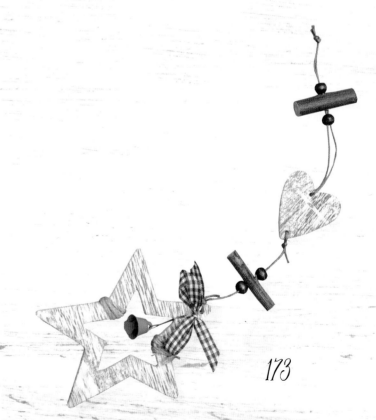

Ham & Leek Risotto

The addition of leeks and peas makes this speedy risotto a satisfying family meal, and is a perfect way of using up the Christmas ham.

SERVES 4   PREP 20 MINS   COOK 35 MINS

380 g/13¼ oz arborio rice

1 litre/1¾ pints water

1 shallot

2 leeks, white and light green parts only

350 g/12 oz cooked ham

25 g/1 oz fresh parsley, plus extra to garnish

2 tbsp olive oil

4 tbsp dry white wine

1 litre/1¾ pints chicken stock, plus extra if needed

145 g/5¼ oz fresh or frozen peas

25 g/1 oz butter

60 g/2¼ oz freshly grated Parmesan cheese, plus extra to garnish

salt and pepper (optional)

1. Place the rice in a large saucepan with the water and a generous pinch of salt, if using. Bring to the boil over a high heat, then reduce the heat to low and simmer, uncovered, for 7 minutes. Meanwhile, dice the shallot and trim and dice the leeks. Dice the ham. Finely chop the parsley. Drain the rice in a colander and set aside.

2. Heat the oil in the pan used to cook the rice. Add the ham, shallot and leeks and cook, stirring, for about 3 minutes until the vegetables begin to soften and the ham begins to brown. Add the wine and cook for a further 1–2 minutes. Add the rice, stock and ¼–½ teaspoon of salt, if using, and bring to the boil. Reduce the heat to medium and simmer, stirring occasionally, for 12 minutes, or until most of the stock has evaporated.

3. Taste the risotto. If it is not yet cooked through, add a little more stock and cook for a few more minutes. Stir in the peas in the last couple of minutes of cooking. Stir the butter and cheese into the risotto. Garnish with cheese and parsley and serve immediately.

Ham & Mushroom Quiche

Quiche is a tasty way of using up leftovers – it can be eaten hot or cold, so is a good solution for those unstructured days after Christmas.

SERVES 4–6   PREP 30 MINS, PLUS 30 MINS' CHILLING   COOK 45–50 MINS

15 g/½ oz butter

1 small onion, finely chopped

115 g/4 oz closed-cup mushrooms, sliced

140 g/5 oz cooked ham, diced

2 eggs, beaten

200 ml/7 fl oz single cream

55 g/2 oz Gruyère cheese, grated

salt and pepper (optional)

PASTRY

200 g/7 oz plain flour

100 g/3½ oz butter

2–3 tbsp cold water

10 g/¼ oz flour, for dusting

1. To make the pastry, sift the flour into a bowl and rub in the butter with your fingertips until the mixture resembles fine breadcrumbs. Stir in just enough water to bind the mixture to a soft dough.

2. Roll out the dough on a lightly floured work surface and use to line a 23-cm/9-inch flan tin. Press into the edges, trim the excess and prick the base with a fork. Chill in the refrigerator for 15 minutes.

3. Preheat the oven to 200°C/400°F/Gas Mark 6. Line the base with a piece of greaseproof paper and fill with baking beans, then blind-bake in the preheated oven for 10 minutes until lightly browned. Remove from the oven and take out the greaseproof paper and beans, then bake for a further 10 minutes.

4. Melt the butter in a frying pan, add the onion and fry for 2 minutes, then add the mushrooms and fry, stirring, for a further 2–3 minutes. Add the ham, then spread the mixture evenly in the pastry case.

5. Put the eggs into a bowl with the cream and beat together, then season to taste with salt and pepper, if using. Pour into the pastry case and sprinkle with the cheese. Bake for 20–25 minutes until golden brown and just set.

Smoked Salmon Risotto

Smoked salmon is something usually eaten cold, but it also works very well in hot dishes – this tasty risotto makes a little go a long way.

| SERVES 4 | PREP 20 MINS | COOK 15–20 MINS |

50 g/1¾ oz unsalted butter

1 onion, finely chopped

½ small fennel bulb, very finely chopped

500 g/1 lb 2 oz arborio rice

300 ml/10 fl oz white wine

1.2 litres/2 pints hot fish stock

150 g/5½ oz hot-smoked salmon flakes

150 g/5½ oz smoked salmon slices

2 tbsp fresh chervil leaves or chopped flat-leaf parsley

salt and pepper (optional)

1. Melt half the butter in a large saucepan over a medium heat, add the onion and fennel and cook, stirring frequently, for 5–8 minutes until transparent and soft. Add the rice and stir well to coat the grains in the butter. Cook, stirring, for 3 minutes, then add the wine, stir and leave to simmer until most of the liquid has been absorbed.

2. With the stock simmering in a separate saucepan, add a ladleful to the rice and stir well. Cook, stirring constantly, until nearly all the liquid has been absorbed, then add another ladleful of stock. Continue to add the remaining stock in the same way until the rice is cooked but still firm to the bite and most or all of the stock has been added.

3. Remove from the heat and stir in the smoked salmon flakes and slices and the remaining butter. Season to taste with salt and pepper, if using, sprinkle over the chervil and serve immediately.

Salmon & Potato Casserole

If you have Brussels sprouts left after Christmas dinner, this is a delicious way to use them with salmon fillets.

SERVES 4–6   PREP 30 MINS   COOK 20 MINS

1 tbsp olive oil, for oiling
450 g/1 lb new potatoes
2 tbsp olive oil
1 tsp salt
350 g/12 oz Brussels sprouts
½ tsp pepper
675 g/1 lb 8 oz salmon fillet
2 tbsp unsalted butter
1 tbsp fresh dill
juice of 1 lemon
3 spring onions

1. Preheat the oven to 230°C/450°F/Gas Mark 8 and oil a large baking dish. Slice the potatoes into thin rounds and place them in the base of the dish in an even layer. Drizzle half the oil evenly over the potatoes, then sprinkle with half the salt. Place in the preheated oven.

2. Meanwhile, trim and thinly slice the sprouts. Put them into a medium-sized bowl and toss with the remaining oil, half the remaining salt and the pepper. Remove the dish from the oven and spread the sliced sprouts over the top of the potatoes in an even layer. Return to the oven. Cut the salmon into 5-cm/2-inch chunks and season with the remaining salt. Put the butter into a small bowl and melt in the microwave. Finely chop the dill and add it to the butter with the lemon juice. Trim and slice the spring onions.

3. Remove the dish from the oven and place the salmon pieces on top of the vegetables. Spoon the butter mixture over the salmon pieces and drizzle any remaining mixture over the vegetables. Scatter the spring onions over the top. Return to the oven and bake for 10–12 minutes until the salmon flakes easily with a fork and is cooked through. Serve immediately.

French Bean Casserole

Make use of any leftover beans with this tasty casserole. Teamed with canned mushroom soup this is a great standby after Christmas.

SERVES 4–6	PREP 10 MINS	COOK 40–45 MINS

500 g/1 lb 2 oz French beans, cut into 4-cm/1½-inch lengths

300 ml/10 fl oz canned condensed mushroom soup

225 ml/8 fl oz milk

1 tsp soy sauce

1 tbsp corn oil

15 g/½ oz butter

1 onion, sliced into rings

1. Preheat the oven to 180°C/350°F/Gas Mark 4. Bring a saucepan of water to the boil and add the beans. Bring back to the boil and cook for 5 minutes. Drain well.

2. Put the soup, milk and soy sauce into a bowl and mix together, then stir in the beans. Tip into a 1.5-litre/2½-pint casserole and distribute evenly. Bake in the preheated oven for 25–30 minutes, until bubbling and golden.

3. Meanwhile, heat the oil and butter in a frying pan, add the onion rings and fry over a fairly high heat, stirring frequently, until golden brown and crisp. Remove and drain on absorbent kitchen paper.

4. Arrange the onion rings on top of the casserole and bake for a further 5 minutes. Serve hot.

Mushroom Stroganoff

A delicious vegetarian spin on the original beef stroganoff, this is quick to prepare and will use up any mushrooms you may have left.

SERVES 4	PREP 10 MINS	COOK 15–20 MINS

25 g/1 oz butter

1 onion, finely chopped

450 g/1 lb closed-cup mushrooms, quartered

1 tsp tomato purée

1 tsp wholegrain mustard

150 ml/5 fl oz crème fraîche

1 tsp paprika, plus extra to garnish

salt and pepper (optional)

fresh flat-leaf parsley sprigs, to garnish

1. Heat the butter in a large, heavy-based frying pan. Add the onion and cook gently for 5–10 minutes until soft.

2. Add the mushrooms to the pan and stir-fry for a few minutes until they begin to soften.

3. Stir in the tomato purée and mustard, then add the crème fraîche. Cook gently, stirring constantly, for 5 minutes.

4. Stir in the paprika and season with salt and pepper, if using, then garnish with parsley and serve immediately.

❄ Variation ❄

IF YOU PREFER TO BE COMPLETELY AUTHENTIC, YOU COULD USE THE MORE TRADITIONAL SOURED CREAM IN PLACE OF THE CRÈME FRAÎCHE.

From the Christmas Kitchen

* * * * * *

Indulgent Peppermint Hot Chocolate Mix

Peppermint crisp chocolate adds great flavour and a splash of colour to a classic festive treat – make a batch and give as a gift.

MAKES 6	PREP 10 MINS	COOK NONE

690 g/1 lb 8¾ oz milk powder

125 g/4½ oz cocoa powder

300 g/10½ oz sugar

250 g/9 oz peppermint crisp chocolate, chopped

1. You will need six 475-ml/16-fl oz wide-mouthed preserving jars for this recipe. To prepare the gift jars, divide all of the ingredients evenly between the jars. Add the ingredients in layers, starting with the milk powder. Place the lids on the jars and secure tightly.

2. Attach a tag to each jar with these instructions:

How to prepare Indulgent Peppermint Hot Chocolate
Pour the contents of the jar into a medium-sized bowl and mix to combine. For each serving, put 40 g/1½ oz of the mix into a mug and add 175 ml/6 fl oz hot water or milk. Stir until the mix is completely dissolved. Serve immediately.

Tip

THE HOT CHOCOLATE MIX WILL KEEP FOR UP TO 6 MONTHS. COVER TIGHTLY AND STORE IN A COOL, DRY PLACE.

Whisky Fudge

If you know a chocolate and whisky lover, this is the perfect treat for them. You can use a good brandy instead of whisky, if you prefer.

SERVES 16   PREP 15 MINS   COOK 10–15 MINS, PLUS SETTING

1 tbsp sunflower oil, for oiling

250 g/9 oz soft brown sugar

100 g/3½ oz unsalted butter, diced

400 g/14 oz canned sweetened full-fat condensed milk

2 tbsp glucose syrup

150 g/5½ oz plain chocolate, roughly chopped

60 ml/2¼ fl oz whisky

25 g/1 oz walnut pieces

1. Lightly brush a 20-cm/8-inch square baking tin with oil. Line it with non-stick baking paper, snipping diagonally into the corners, then pressing the paper into the tin so that the base and sides are lined.

2. Put the sugar, butter, condensed milk and glucose syrup into a heavy-based saucepan. Heat gently, stirring, until the sugar has dissolved.

3. Increase the heat, bring to the boil and boil for 12–15 minutes, or until the mixture reaches 116°C/240°F on a sugar thermometer (if you don't have a sugar thermometer, spoon a little of the syrup into some iced water; it will form a soft ball when it is ready). As the temperature rises, stir the fudge occasionally so the sugar doesn't stick and burn. Remove the fudge from the heat. Add the chocolate and whisky and stir together until the chocolate has melted and the mixture is smooth.

4. Preheat the grill to medium–hot. Put the walnuts on a baking tray and toast them under the grill for 2–3 minutes, or until browned. Roughly chop them.

5. Pour the mixture into the prepared tin, smooth the surface using a spatula and sprinkle over the walnuts. Leave to cool for 1 hour. Cover with clingfilm, then chill in the refrigerator for 1–2 hours, or until firm. Lift the fudge out of the tin, peel off the paper and cut into small squares. Store in an airtight container in a cool, dry place for up to 2 weeks.

189

Espresso Truffles

The delicate, edible gold leaf on these tasty truffles makes them an extra special gift for any chocoholic.

300 g/10½ oz plain chocolate, roughly chopped

2 tbsp double cream

1 tbsp strong espresso coffee, cooled

2 tbsp coffee liqueur

55 g/2 oz unsalted butter, softened and diced

edible gold leaf, to decorate (optional)

1. Put 100 g/3½ oz of the chocolate and all the cream into a heatproof bowl set over a saucepan of gently simmering water and heat, stirring, until the chocolate is melted.

2. Remove from the heat, add the coffee, coffee liqueur and butter and whisk for 3–4 minutes, or until thickened. Transfer to an airtight container and chill in the refrigerator for 6–8 hours, or until firm.

3. Line a baking tray with non-stick baking paper. Scoop out teaspoons of the mixture and roll them into truffle-sized balls. Place the balls on the prepared tray, cover with clingfilm and freeze for 6–8 hours.

4. Put the remaining chocolate into a heatproof bowl set over a saucepan of gently simmering water and heat until melted. Using two forks, dip each truffle into the chocolate to coat evenly. Return to the prepared tray and chill in the refrigerator for 1–2 hours, or until firm. Top each truffle with edible gold leaf to decorate, if using. Store in an airtight container in the refrigerator for up to 5 days.

Pistachio & Apricot Nougat

Delicious home-made nougat, with pistachios and dried apricots, is the perfect gift for anyone with a sweet tooth.

SERVES 16	PREP 30 MINS, PLUS SETTING	COOK 15 MINS

edible rice paper
250 g/9 oz caster sugar
125 ml/4 fl oz liquid glucose
85 g/3 oz clear honey
2 tbsp water
pinch of salt
1 egg white
½ tsp vanilla extract
60 g/2¼ oz unsalted butter, softened and diced
50 g/1¾ oz pistachio nuts, roughly chopped
50 g/1¾ oz ready-to-eat dried apricots, finely chopped

1. Line a 17-cm/7-inch square loose-based cake tin with clingfilm, leaving an overhang. Line the base with a piece of the rice paper.

2. Put the sugar, glucose, honey, water and salt into a heavy-based saucepan. Heat gently until the sugar has dissolved, tilting the pan to mix the ingredients together. Increase the heat, bring to the boil and boil for 8 minutes, or until the mixture reaches 121°C/250°F on a sugar thermometer.

3. Whisk the egg white in a clean, greasefree bowl until firm. Gradually pour in a quarter of the hot syrup in a thin stream while still beating the egg. Continue beating for 5 minutes, until the mixture is stiff enough to hold its shape on the whisk.

4. Put the pan containing the remaining syrup over a low heat for 2 minutes, or until the mixture reaches 143°C/290°F on a sugar thermometer. Gradually pour the syrup over the egg mixture while beating.

5. Add the vanilla extract and butter and beat for a further 5 minutes. Add the pistachio nuts and apricots and stir.

6. Pour the mixture into the tin and level with a palette knife. Cover with rice paper and chill in the refrigerator for 8–10 hours, or until fairly firm.

7. Lift the nougat out of the tin and cut into 16 squares. Store in an airtight container in the refrigerator for up to 5 days.

Double Chocolate Brownie Mix

This beats a packet brownie mix any day. It makes a great gift, which takes away most of the work and leaves all of the pleasure.

MAKES 6	PREP 10 MINS	COOK NONE

750 g/1 lb 10 oz plain flour

1½ tsp salt

600 g/1 lb 5 oz soft light brown sugar

800 g/1 lb 12 oz granulated sugar

350 g/12 oz cocoa powder

450 g/1 lb toasted hazelnuts, chopped

525 g/1 lb 3 oz mini plain chocolate chips

1. You will need six 475-ml/16-fl oz wide-mouthed preserving jars for this recipe. To prepare the gift jars, divide all of the ingredients evenly between the jars. Add the ingredients in layers, starting with the flour. Place the lids on the jars and secure tightly.

2. Attach a gift tag to each jar with these instructions:

How to prepare Double Chocolate Brownies

You will need:

2 large eggs

2 tbsp milk

1 tsp vanilla extract

115 g/4 oz butter, melted, plus extra for greasing

Preheat the oven to 180°C/350°F/Gas Mark 4 and grease a 23 x 33-cm/9 x 13-inch rectangular cake tin.

Transfer the brownie mix from the jar to a large mixing bowl. Put the eggs, milk and vanilla extract into a separate bowl and mix to combine. Add the egg mixture to the dry ingredients and mix until well combined. Stir in the melted butter and mix to combine.

Transfer the batter to the prepared tin and bake in the preheated oven for about 20 minutes, until the top is dry and a cocktail stick inserted into the centre comes out almost clean. Place the tin on a wire rack and leave to cool completely. Serve at room temperature.

Christmas Ginger Thins

These spicy ginger thins will not only tickle your recipients' taste buds, but will fill their homes with the festive aroma of freshly baked cookies.

500 g/1 lb 2 oz plain flour

2 tsp bicarbonate of soda

1 tsp salt

2 tbsp ground ginger

2 tsp ground cinnamon

1 tsp ground cloves

345 g/11¾ oz unsalted butter, at room temperature

200 g/7 oz granulated sugar

200 g/7 oz soft dark brown sugar

2 large eggs

245 g/8¾ oz treacle

400 g/14 oz coarse brown sugar

1. You will need six 475-ml/16-fl oz wide-mouthed preserving jars for this recipe. Line two large baking sheets with baking paper.

2. Put the flour, bicarbonate of soda, salt, ginger, cinnamon and cloves into a medium-sized bowl and mix to combine.

3. Put the butter, granulated sugar and soft dark brown sugar into a large bowl and beat until light and fluffy. Add the eggs and treacle and mix until incorporated. Add the flour mixture and beat until incorporated, scraping down the side of the bowl once or twice.

4. Put the coarse brown sugar in a shallow bowl. Shape the dough into 4-cm/1½-inch balls and roll in the sugar to coat completely. Place the balls on the prepared baking sheet spaced well apart. When the first sheet is full, use your fingertips to flatten the balls into rounds about 7.5 cm/3 inches in diameter (they should be about the same diameter as the preserving jars) and 2.5 mm/⅛ inch thick. If your fingers become too sticky, dip them in the sugar. Place the sheet in the freezer. Continue to shape the remaining dough until all the dough has been used and both sheets are full. Place the second sheet in the freezer and freeze for at least 4 hours or overnight, until the cookies are completely frozen.

5. Stack 12 frozen cookies in each of the six jars. Attach a gift tag to each jar with these instructions:

How to bake Christmas Ginger Thins

Keep frozen until required. Preheat the oven to 180°C/350°F/Gas Mark 4 and place the cookies on an ungreased baking sheet. Bake in the preheated oven for 12–14 minutes, until the cookies are dry on the top and beginning to crisp. Remove from the oven and transfer to a wire rack to cool completely. Serve at room temperature.

Vanilla Fudge

Just a few simple ingredients and you can make the creamiest vanilla fudge ever, perfect for a Christmas treat.

MAKES 16   PREP 15 MINS, PLUS SETTING   COOK 15–20 MINS

1 tbsp sunflower oil, for oiling

450 g/1 lb caster sugar

85 g/3 oz unsalted butter

150 ml/5 fl oz milk

150 ml/5 fl oz canned evaporated milk

2 tsp vanilla extract

1. Lightly brush a 20-cm/8-inch square baking tin with oil. Line it with non-stick baking paper, snipping diagonally into the corners, then pressing the paper into the tin so that the base and sides are lined.

2. Put the sugar, butter, milk and evaporated milk into a heavy-based saucepan. Heat gently, stirring, until the sugar has dissolved.

3. Increase the heat, bring to the boil and boil for 12–15 minutes, or until the mixture reaches 116°C/240°F on a sugar thermometer (if you don't have a sugar thermometer, spoon a little of the syrup into some iced water; it will form a soft ball when it is ready). As the temperature rises, stir the fudge occasionally so the sugar doesn't stick and burn.

4. Remove the pan from the heat, add the vanilla extract and beat with a wooden spoon until thickened.

5. Pour the mixture into the prepared tin and smooth the surface with a spatula. Leave to cool for 1 hour until set.

6. Lift the fudge out of the tin, peel off the paper and cut into small squares. Store in an airtight container in a cool, dry place for up to 2 weeks.

Nutty Peppermint Bark

Kids and adults alike will love this treat. If you can't get hold of peppermint candy canes, substitute them with any hard mint sweets.

MAKES 25   *PREP 20 MINS, PLUS CHILLING*   *COOK 3–4 MINS*

200 g/7 oz red-and-white striped peppermint candy canes, broken into pieces

500 g/1 lb 2 oz white chocolate, roughly chopped

100 g/3½ oz chopped mixed nuts

1. Line a 30 x 20-cm/12 x 8-inch baking tin with non-stick baking paper.

2. Put the broken candy canes into a large polythene food bag and seal tightly. Using a rolling pin, bash the bag until the canes are crushed into small pieces.

3. Put the chocolate into a heatproof bowl set over a saucepan of gently simmering water and heat until melted. Remove from the heat and stir in three quarters of the crushed candy canes.

4. Pour the mixture into the prepared tin, smooth the surface using a spatula and sprinkle over the chopped nuts and remaining candy. Press down very slightly to ensure they stick. Cover with clingfilm and chill in the refrigerator for 30 minutes, or until firm.

5. Break the peppermint bark into small, uneven pieces. Store in an airtight container in a cool, dry place for up to 2 weeks.

Mixed Nuts in Herbed Salt

Simple to make and wonderfully tasty, these moreish pan-roasted nuts are bursting with protein, healthy fats and lots of flavour.

SERVES 4	PREP 10 MINS, PLUS COOLING	COOK 5 MINS

1 tbsp olive oil

2 fresh rosemary sprigs, leaves torn from the stems

55 g/2 oz cashew nuts

55 g/2 oz pecan nuts

55 g/2 oz unblanched almonds

55 g/2 oz unblanched hazelnuts

½ tsp sea salt

1. Heat the oil and rosemary in a frying pan, then swirl the oil around the pan to infuse with the rosemary. Add the nuts and cook for 2–3 minutes until lightly toasted.

2. Stir in the salt, then spoon the nuts into a bowl and leave to cool. Any leftover nuts can be stored in the refrigerator in a plastic container or preserving jar for up to 3 days.

❄ Variation ❄

TRY REPLACING THE ROSEMARY WITH A LITTLE CURRY POWDER OR A BLEND OF GROUND TURMERIC, GARAM MASALA, SMOKED PAPRIKA AND A PINCH OF CHILLI.

198

Corn Relish

This golden relish will be a very popular Christmas gift – it can be served with roast meat or salad and it has a long fridge life.

MAKES 600 G/1 LB 5 OZ	PREP 10 MINS, PLUS COOLING	COOK 30 MINS

5 corn cobs,
about 900 g/2 lb, husked

1 red pepper, deseeded and
finely diced

2 celery sticks,
very finely chopped

1 red onion, finely chopped

125 g/4½ oz sugar

1 tbsp salt

2 tbsp mustard powder

½ tsp celery seeds

**small pinch of
turmeric (optional)**

225 ml/8 fl oz cider vinegar

125 ml/4 fl oz water

1. Bring a large saucepan of water to the boil and fill a bowl with iced water. Add the corn to the boiling water, bring back to the boil and cook for 2 minutes, or until the kernels are tender-crisp. Using tongs, immediately plunge the cobs into the cold water to halt cooking. Remove from the water and cut the kernels from the cobs, then set aside.

2. Add the red pepper, celery and onion to the corn cooking water, bring back to the boil and boil for 2 minutes, or until tender-crisp. Drain well and return to the pan with the corn kernels.

3. Put the sugar, salt, mustard powder, celery seeds and turmeric, if using, into a bowl and mix together, then stir in the vinegar and water. Add to the pan, bring the liquid to the boil, then reduce the heat and simmer for 15 minutes, stirring occasionally.

4. Ladle the relish into hot, sterilized preserving jars, filling them to within 1 cm/½ inch of the top of each jar. Wipe the rims and secure the lids. Leave the relish to cool completely, then refrigerate for up to 2 months.

Christmas Crafts

* * * * * *

Handmade Stocking

Fill this cute little Christmas stocking with gifts and it will look perfect hanging from the mantelpiece. It requires very simple sewing skills.

two 25 x 30 cm/10 x 12 inches pressed, 100% wool felt sheets, 4 mm/⅛ inch thick

contrasting cotton fabric offcuts

matching or co-ordinating embroidery thread

YOU WILL ALSO NEED

a large piece of paper, scissors, pins, sharp fabric scissors, pinking shears, darning needle

1. Enlarge the Christmas Stocking and Christmas Tree for Stocking templates on page 221 on a photocopier to the required size. The finished stocking for this project is 28 cm/11 inches in height, but you can vary this size. Copy and cut out the following templates: two stocking shapes and one Christmas tree.

2. Make the following templates using a large piece of paper: two rectangular cuff shapes, measuring 23 cm/9 inches long by 10 cm/4 inches wide and one rectangular loop shape, measuring 30 cm/12 inches long by 6cm/2½ inches wide.

3. Pin the stocking template to the felt fabric and cut out using the fabric scissors. As the felt fabric is the same on both sides, there is no need to worry about turning the template over.

4. Pin the cuff templates, tree and loop to the contrasting cotton fabric and cut out using the pinking shears.

5. Thread the darning needle with a length of embroidery thread and tie a knot in the end. Use the same embroidery thread for all of the sewing.

6. Place the Christmas tree shape on top of one of the felt stocking shapes, so that the foot of the stocking is facing left and the pattern of the Christmas tree is the right way around. Secure the thread to the back of the stocking shape and sew the Christmas tree on top of the felt, using a very simple running stitch.

7. The cuff template is much bigger than the width of the stocking to allow the edges of the cuff to be folded around the top of the stocking. Place the felt stocking shape, Christmas tree showing, on top of the inside of the cuff shape. Fold half of the fabric over the top of the stocking, making sure that the material is the right way around if there is a pattern. Fold the edges of the cuff to the inside of the stocking and, using a simple running stitch, sew each edge of the cuff to the stocking along the sides. Leave the pinking shear edge unattached at the front.

8. Place both pieces of the stocking together. Use a simple running stitch to sew around the edges of the stocking, leaving the top cuffed edge open.

9. Fold the loop shape in half lengthways, making sure that the pattern is on the outside, and sew along the length using running stitch. Leave the pinked edge showing. Form a loop and place each end inside the stocking at the top right-hand side of the cuff. Sew each end of the loop to the inside of the stocking using running stitch. Check all pins have been removed before hanging up for Christmas.

Decorative Jars

These tealight holders cast a festive shadow of snowflakes. Vary the size of the jars and the colour of the snowflakes to create a magical atmosphere.

assorted glass jars in various shapes and sizes

small snowflake-shaped paper punch

white tissue paper

craft glue

crochet snowflakes

assorted festive ribbons, cut into 50-cm/20-inch lengths

battery-operated tealights

YOU WILL ALSO NEED

glue spreader or stiff paintbrush

1. Wash the glass jars in mild soapy water to make sure they are free of grease.

2. Using a snowflake-shaped paper punch, stamp out a selection of tissue paper snowflakes. Use a glue spreader or stiff paintbrush to apply glue to the entire surface of one of the jars. Place the tissue paper snowflakes on the layer of glue in a random pattern. Apply a layer of glue over the top of them. Set the covered jar to one side to dry. Don't worry if the jar looks white, craft glue will dry clear.

3. Cover one side of a crochet snowflake with a generous coating of glue and attach it to another jar. Choose either two larger crochet snowflakes or a selection of smaller crochet snowflakes to attach to more jars in a random pattern.

4. Leave the finished jars to dry for about 3 hours.

5. When the jars are completely dry, tie a selection of ribbons around the neck of the jar, switch on the tealights and place inside.

Tip SAVE JAM JARS AND PICKLE JARS TO MAKE UP A SELECTION OF DIFFERENT SIZED JARS. USE PAPER LACE DOILIES TO GLUE TO THE JARS INSTEAD OF THE PAPER SNOWFLAKES AND EXPERIMENT WITH SEVERAL COLOURS OF TISSUE PAPER TO VARY THE LIGHT CAST FROM THE JARS.

Angel Card Tree Decoration

This delightful card design incorporates a balsa wood angel that can be removed from the card to hang on the Christmas tree.

300-gsm white card

gold paper

small and large-weave hessian

scrap card

board 2 mm/¹⁄₁₆ inch thick

balsa wood 3 mm/
⅛ inch thick

white and cadmium yellow
acrylic paints

gold enamel paint

thin craft wire

YOU WILL ALSO NEED

craft knife, steel-edged
ruler, cutting mat, pencil,
scoring tool, double-sided
tape, black felt-tip pen,
paintbrush, long-nosed
pliers, superglue, pin

1. Using a craft knife and steel-edged ruler on a cutting mat, cut a piece of the white card 15.5 x 19 cm/6⅛ x 7½ inches. Score down the centre with a scoring tool and fold in half. Attach the gold paper to the front of the folded card with double-sided tape. Trim with the craft knife and steel-edged ruler. Cut a 15.5 x 9.5-cm/6⅛ x 3¾-inch piece of small-weave hessian. Use an existing frayed edge for the right-hand edge or fray by pulling a few vertical strands away. Attach the hessian with double-sided tape so that it fits exactly over the gold paper.

2. Enlarge the templates on page 221 on a photocopier as directed and cut out. Draw around the templates on scrap card and cut out with a craft knife and steel-edged ruler on a cutting mat.

3. Draw around the angel silhouette onto the large-weave hessian with the black felt-tip pen and cut out. Attach to the card with double-sided tape.

4. Using the template, cut a large heart from gold paper and attach it to a piece of board with double-sided tape, then attach to the hessian angel. Open the card and lay flat, then cut a small upside-down 'V' in the top edge of the card front. This will serve as a hook for the balsa wood angel.

5. Using the templates and craft knife, cut the wings, angel body and a small heart from balsa wood. Paint the head and wings with white acrylic paint. Add a tiny amount of yellow to the white to make a cream for the dress. While drying, paint the heart with gold enamel paint. Cut a 13-cm/ 5-inch length of wire with the pliers and twist the ends together for a length of 1 cm/½ inch, forming a hoop for the halo.

6. Paint white polka dots on the dress. When dry, superglue the angel body to the wings, and the heart to the body. Use the pin to make a hole at the top of the wings behind the angel's back. Superglue the twisted wire of the halo into the hole.

Christmas Snowflake Card

Just one template can be used to create four classy card designs that will look stunning on display in the home.

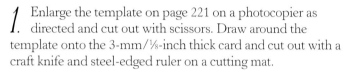

3-mm/⅛-inch thick card

300-gsm Bockingford (slightly textured) paper

300-gsm white card

silver and/or gold spray paint

silver and/or gold card

YOU WILL ALSO NEED

scissors, pencil, craft knife, steel-edged ruler, cutting mat, masking tape, bone folder, double-sided tape, old newspaper, face mask and protective gloves

1. Enlarge the template on page 221 on a photocopier as directed and cut out with scissors. Draw around the template onto the 3-mm/⅛-inch thick card and cut out with a craft knife and steel-edged ruler on a cutting mat.

2. Place the template on the Bockingford paper and secure with masking tape. Ensure there is enough space to create a 15-cm/6-inch square. Turn the paper over and rub firmly all over the template area with a bone folder to create an impression.

3. Remove the template. Ensure that the embossed snowflake is in the centre of the paper, then trim to 15 cm/6 inches square.

4. Cut a 15 x 30-cm/6 x 12-inch piece of white card. Score down the centre with a bone folder and fold in half. Use double-sided tape around the edges of the embossed snowflake panel to attach it to the card.

5. Repeat steps 2–4 to create a second card, but attach the Bockingford paper to the opposite side of the white card to create a reversed impression.

6. To make a third card, place the template on the front of folded white card (see step 4). Protect your work surface with old newspaper. Wearing a face mask and protective gloves, spray silver and/or gold paint over the card. When dry, remove the template to reveal the snowflake.

7. To make a fourth card, cut a 15 x 30-cm/6 x 12-inch piece of silver or gold card. Score down the centre with a bone folder and fold in half. Respray the snowflake template so that it contrasts with the card, if needed, and attach it to the card front with double-sided tape.

Christmas Wreath

You won't need special floristry skills to create this simple indoor decoration. Vary the patterns, colours and ribbons for different occasions.

20 metres/65 feet assorted ribbons of various widths with a Christmas theme

10 metres/32 feet natural jute hessian ribbon, 2.5 cm/ 1 inch wide

25-cm/10-inch round flat wire wreath frame

YOU WILL ALSO NEED

fabric scissors, ruler or tape measure

1. Cut various lengths between 25–35 cm/10–14 inches from the assorted and jute hessian ribbons, using a ruler or tape measure as a guide. Don't worry about being too precise, this design looks more effective with materials of various lengths.

2. Tie the first piece of ribbon in a bow around the wire frame. The aim is to fill the entire frame with ribbon bows, so start anywhere with the first one. Again, don't worry about being too neat, the aim is for a rustic, shabby-chic look.

3. Use different lengths, colours and patterns of ribbon and continue to tie bows all the way around the frame, alternating between the jute hessian and other ribbons as you progress. Gently push each bow towards the previous bow to make sure there isn't any of the wire frame visible.

4. Once you have filled the entire frame, tie a final length of ribbon around the frame to create a loop for hanging the wreath. The wreath works both ways when you hang it, so turn it around for two styles in one.

❄ *Tip* ❄

THE SIZE OF THE WREATH IS ADAPTABLE. SIMPLY BUY A SMALLER OR LARGER FLAT WIRE WREATH FRAME AND ADJUST THE QUANTITY OF RIBBON OR FABRIC. PURCHASE FRAMES FROM A LOCAL FLORIST OR ONLINE.

Gift Tags & Gift Decorations

Add a touch of vintage chic to your Christmas presents with these elegant gift tags. You can vary the lacy design with a variety of paper doilies.

medium-weight brown kraft card

paper doilies with a scalloped edge

hole punch reinforcers (optional)

thin silver ribbon or twine, cut into 15–20-cm/6–8-inch lengths

YOU WILL ALSO NEED

paper, scissors, pencil, hole punch, glue stick

1. Create templates on paper to your chosen size and cut out. Rectangles approximately 9cm/3½ inches long by 6 cm/2½ inches wide, and circles 6cm/2½ inches in diameter work well for this.

2. Draw around the template onto the brown kraft card and cut out with a pair of scissors.

3. Punch a hole in the top of the gift tag. Apply a layer of glue to the bottom half of the tag with the glue stick.

4. Place one of the lace edges of a paper doily onto the layer of glue on the bottom half of the tag. Choose a symmetrical section of the doily so the scalloped edge becomes a feature of the tag. Trim the doily around the edges of the gift tag.

5. Apply the hole reinforcers, if using. Thread a length of ribbon or twine through the hole and knot it to create a tie for your tag.

Tip VARY THE COLOUR OF THE CARD TO CREATE A VARIETY OF GIFT TAGS TO COMPLEMENT YOUR WRAPPING PAPER.

Christmas Card Tree Decorations

If you'd like to give something more than a card, but you are not sure of what to buy, this clever card doubles up as a stylish tree decoration.

300-gsm brown card

pale-green plain paper

brown glitter card

brown corrugated card

8-cm/3¼-inch length of 5-mm/¼-inch wide red ribbon

pale-green handmade paper

12-cm/4½-inch length of 2-mm/¹⁄₁₆-inch wide green ribbon

small deep-red glass bead

YOU WILL ALSO NEED

pencil, craft knife, steel-edged ruler, cutting mat, scoring tool, hole punch, glue stick, double-sided tape

1. Enlarge the template on page 220 on a photocopier to the required size and cut out. Draw around the template on the brown card and cut out with a craft knife and steel-edged ruler on a cutting mat. Score down the centre with a scoring tool and fold. Punch a hole near the top.

2. Cover the inside of the tree with glue stick. Stick the plain green paper on one half of the inside, placing it down the centre fold and making sure it adheres well. Trim with the craft knife. Repeat on the opposite side. Cut out the punched hole with the craft knife.

3. Cut a trunk from brown glitter card and attach in two pieces to the front and back of the card with double-sided tape. Cut the container from brown corrugated card and attach in the same way.

4. Attach the red ribbon with double-sided tape, running it over the card spine.

5. Use a glue stick to adhere the green handmade-quality paper in one piece to the front and back of the outside of the card. Cut out the punched hole. Create a loop for hanging from the green ribbon, threading the deep-red glass bead on to it before tying off.

Decorative Centrepiece

Bring some sparkle to your festive feast with this special table centrepiece. Have fun collecting old buttons and vintage ribbon for this project.

old newspaper

fir cones in a variety of shapes and sizes

snow spray

glass cookie jar

mini LED battery-operated lights

20–30 gold sequins

1 metre/39 inches jute burlap ribbon, at least 1 cm/½ inch thick

YOU WILL ALSO NEED

protective mask and gloves, craft glue

1. In a well-ventilated room, lay the newspaper on a flat surface and spread out the fir cones. Using a protective mask and gloves, spray the fir cones with the snow spray, turning the cones around to make sure that all parts are covered with a light coating. Leave to dry for about 30 minutes.

2. Once the cones are dry, place an initial selection of cones in the base of the glass cookie jar. Twist the first section of the LED mini lights around the fir cones and start adding more cones to the jar, twisting the lights around them as you fill the jar up. When you get to the top of the jar, carefully disguise the battery section of the LED lights in the middle of the fir cones, making sure you can still get access to switch them on.

3. Stick sequins to the ends of the jute burlap ribbon in a random pattern, using blobs of craft glue. Once the glue has completely dried and the sequins are securely attached, place the ribbon around the top of the jar and tie in a bow.

4. Turn the lights on and replace the lid of the cookie jar.

Country-style Garland

Perfect for creating a country cottage feel, this will bring traditional festive cheer to your home. Make short ones or a few longer ones.

small-weave hessian fabric 30 cm/12 inches square

large-weave hessian fabric 30 cm/12 inches square

scraps of pale-green and deep-red felt

scraps of deep-red gingham and plain red cotton fabric

natural string

decorative gold fine thread

5 red buttons, diameter 2 cm/¾ inch

embroidery needle

deep-red embroidery thread

thin craft wire

6 tiny wooden pegs

2 tiny felt hearts

YOU WILL ALSO NEED

scissors, tailor's chalk, craft knife, cutting mat, tape measure, fabric glue, long-nosed pliers, strong double-sided tape

1. Enlarge the templates on page 220 on a photocopier as directed and cut out using scissors. Using tailor's chalk and either scissors or a craft knife on a cutting mat, cut out the following: 2 circles from small-weave hessian, 2 from large-weave hessian; 2 large stars from each hessian, 1 small star from green felt; 4 angel bodies from large-weave hessian; 4 angel wings from small-weave hessian; 2 large hearts from red gingham, 2 from red felt; 2 small hearts from red gingham, 2 from red felt, 2 from green felt.

2. Lay a 1.5-m/59-inch length of string on a work surface and twist the gold thread around. Tie a loop at either end and fray the ends.

3. Cover one side of the buttons with fabric glue and attach the red felt. Cut around the buttons with a craft knife. Pass the needle and thread through the buttonholes once so the thread ends dangle from the back of the button by about 1.5 cm/⅝ inch. Ensure that two of the buttons have extra thread hanging.

4. Arrange the embellishments on the string, working out from the centre. Run a length of thin wire around the top of the red and gingham large hearts with pliers and use double-sided tape to sandwich between the fabrics. Glue a small green heart to the plain red side and add one of the buttons. Use two pegs to attach the string

5. Construct the angels in the same way, but simply sandwich the string in between the head and tops of the wings. Sandwich the wings (two sets per angel) in between the bodies. Glue the tiny felt hearts in place.

6. Construct the remaining embellishments in the same way, using wire to strengthen them, then attach them to the string.

Advent Calendar

Every child knows that the Advent calendar means Christmas isn't too far away. Choose your own treats to fill this delightful calendar.

beige thick cotton fabric
1 metre/39 inches square

red and dark-green felt

roll of matt laminate

2 pieces of bamboo cane
36 cm/14¼ inches in length

bright-red soft thick fabric
62 x 93 cm/25 x 37 inches

sewing needle and deep-red
strong cotton thread

extra-strong iron-on hemming
tape

6 pairs of deep-red baby
socks, age 0–3 months

6 pairs of deep-green baby
socks, age 0–3 months

25 Christmas-tree
embellishments in red,
green and gold

24 tiny wooden pegs

1.5-metres/59 inches of
1-cm/½-inch wide
green ribbon

large silver bell

36-cm/14¼-inch length of
5-mm/¼-inch wide red
ribbon

YOU WILL ALSO NEED

scissors, craft knife, steel-
edged ruler, cutting mat,
pinking shears, tacking
pins, tacking thread, strong
double-sided tape, steam
iron, fabric glue

1. Enlarge the box templates on page 221 on a photocopier as directed and cut out using scissors. Cut 24 large rectangles from the beige fabric using a craft knife and a steel-edged ruler on a cutting mat. Cut 24 small squares from red felt with pinking shears.

2. Use the template to cut the tree from green felt, place on the beige fabric and cut out a slightly larger tree for a border. Laminate the sheet of numbers, then cut out with the craft knife and ruler.

3. Place one length of bamboo at the top of the large piece of red fabric and fold the top edge of the fabric over. Pin, then tack the hem. Hand sew with red thread, then remove the tacking stitches. Repeat at the bottom of the fabric.

4. Temporarily position all the beige squares and the beige tree on the red fabric with double-sided tape, ensuring that they are evenly positioned. Using the iron-on hemming tape around the edges and following the manufacturer's instructions, attach them to the red fabric one row at a time.

5. Using fabric glue, adhere the red felt squares about halfway up and 5 mm/¼ inch in from the right-hand side. Use double-sided tape to attach the numbers centrally to each red square. Attach the green felt tree to the beige tree with fabric glue. Sew the socks to the tops of corners of the beige squares. Open them fully to add your treats, then stick the heels down with fabric glue. Use fabric glue to attach the tree embellishments, ensuring sock number 24 has 2 slightly overlapping trees. Add the pegs to look like they are holding the socks up. Tie bows in the green ribbon, attach the bell and sew to the tree in the bottom right-hand corner.

6. To create hanging loops, use the craft knife to make two horizontal incisions just below the bamboo, wide enough to thread the red ribbon through and under the bamboo. Slightly overlap the ribbon and sew together. Move the ribbon around to hide the sewn part behind the bamboo. Check all pins have been removed before hanging up for Christmas.

Templates

Country-style
Garland (enlarge by 200%)

Christmas Card Tree
Decoration
(enlarge by 200%)

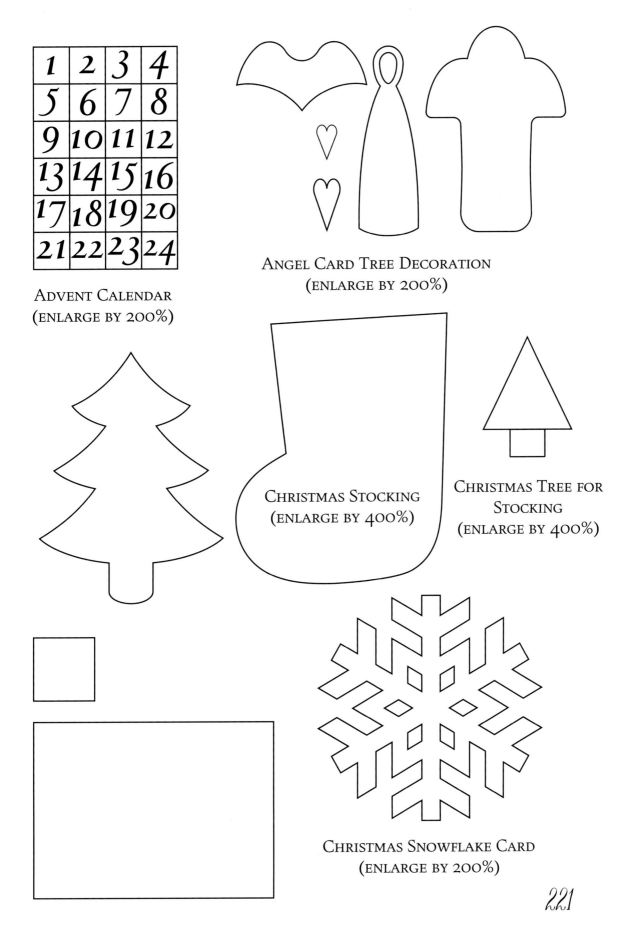

1	2	3	4
5	6	7	8
9	10	11	12
13	14	15	16
17	18	19	20
21	22	23	24

ADVENT CALENDAR
(ENLARGE BY 200%)

ANGEL CARD TREE DECORATION
(ENLARGE BY 200%)

CHRISTMAS STOCKING
(ENLARGE BY 400%)

CHRISTMAS TREE FOR
STOCKING
(ENLARGE BY 400%)

CHRISTMAS SNOWFLAKE CARD
(ENLARGE BY 200%)

Index